EVERYTHING BRIGHT, CLEAR, AND BEAUTIFUL

A YEAR OF POETRY

RACHEL DEVENISH FORD

INTRODUCTION

From March 2020 to March 2021, from my home in Thailand, I wrote one poem for each day.

It's a journey, this book of 365 poems, because the first year of our global pandemic was a journey if it was anything. You can read it in the poems, a mixture of the quiet of lockdown and the rumbling of the times. Poems about going through the racial justice uprisings of the summer with my interracial family are interspersed with learning about virus variants, gardening, and driving my motorbike through villages in our hills.

The book also contains a lot about my own little cast of characters. My husband of twenty years, Chinua, and my children, Kai, Kenya, Leafy, Solomon, and Isaac. At the time I started writing, they were 17, 16, 14, 11, and 7.

Reading back through the poems, I'm so thankful that I had this practice of writing a poem a day. It taught me about consistent small movements toward hope and beauty. It steadied me (and steadies me still, I still do it) and through poetry I was able to tell myself good things. True things.

I hope that you find things in these poems that are true for you, too.

~ Rachel Devenish Ford

MARCH 2020

A FINE COMPANY
March 20

at home, i think the egret and pond heron
who live in our yard
are having a fine time.
all those insects and no one to startle them.
the coucal can flap down from the tallest trees,
sit on the side of the compost bin,
and whoop his hoarse laughter,
the tomatoes have ripened on the vine
rice is in the barn.
we are many miles south
we drove for days to get here,
and we have learned the name
of the bird who cries in the darkness
—nightjar.
in the early hours of the morning,
when i woke up to to the nightjar's calls,
Chinua handed me binoculars
so i could see our new loud friend on the fence post,
calling and calling, without an answer
and this morning lapwings are
swooping through the coconut trees
crying their news to one another
the doves, koels, and magpie robins also
a winged presence, a fine company
undulating motion, feathers and waves of sound.

NINE OF US
March 21

nine of us walked through the coconut grove:
three generations in surgical masks,
looking for a building we did not know.
we had been summoned to a mandatory meeting.
we drifted as people do,
in irregular formation, stopping to look at birds, of course,
gray birds wheeling in a vaguely blue sky.
we rested our eyes on the long lines of a white Brahmin cow,
sand on the ground, in drifts around the trees, old coconut
fronds. sun a little too strong on our heads,
flowers leaning on walls, cascading over old signs.

when we arrived, we signed our names,
drank water out of plastic cups
sat in chairs a few feet apart.
the atmosphere was calm, kind,
and a little confused.
the microphone the man used
alternately too loud and too quiet.
he gave us information about quarantine
and then we were allowed to go.

we walked back home along the beach.
the ice cream seller was out
the waves white along the shore,
more birds, more sand, more sky.

HERE IS WHAT I SAID:
March 22

"it's okay, you didn't do anything wrong.
it's all a lot, we're so many people in a small house,
stepping on each other
closing clear glass doors so that
people run into them
spilling half a liter of milk in the fridge
breaking glasses
leaving towels on the floor
forgetting to put the butter away
and all of it. it's okay, it's emotional—
so much is happening—
and it means we'll each have our moments,
but look at us. we're doing so well."

it's what i said to my mom
after she apologized for some tiny thing
and i had said sorry too many times the day before
to my husband
for something bigger

and i admitted to my son that
i might have gone overboard
when i got annoyed with the way he was acting.

i'm sure you understand this, and you are
doing your best too
and all of us, all of us, are so beautifully,
heartbreakingly ourselves,
trying in our clumsy ways to be good to each other
and then sometimes we are transcendent,
almost winged, as though we could lift off

our
silhouettes outlined in light
brilliant in flight in the late afternoon.

A SOFT LISTENING
MARCH 23

i walked down to the sea
in the heat of the day
and waded into the ocean with
as much dignity as i could manage
with the waves pushing me this way and that.
the water was warm,
and kind,
not quite turquoise, but something close
something softer
filling the eyes and the heart
its sound a rhythm like breathing,
leading to a long, clean line on the horizon.
i shouted words.
"pandemic!" i shouted. "COVID!
lockdown! medical certificate! quarantine!"
i dug deeper. "economy! death!"
the sea didn't change,
no matter how many words i shouted
it was calm and impervious, unchanging,
which was a hard kind of relief.
but i felt a soft listening
a quiet love
an aching sorrow
from somewhere deeper
something higher and wider and more expansive
than even the ocean.

THE LAST ONES
March 24

    tonight we sang.
    my mandolin was out of tune so i didn't play along,
    but i joined in the singing.

    a couple of retired Swedes,
    the last other people remaining
    in this empty community of villas,
    came out onto their porch and watched.
    we didn't know whether they were enjoying it
    or whether it was getting too late
    for a family of nine to sing on the porch,
    sing so loudly and with so much
    clanging of instruments
    and strumming of chords.

    Solomon danced in his chair like a wild thing.
    i wanted it never to end.
    on Friday those other people
    will leave to fly back to Sweden,
    and we will be all alone.
    i hope they liked the singing, but i suppose,
    after they go, we won't have to care.
    although i will wonder whether they got home safely,
    what their quarantine was like,
    what color their sheets are,
    what they can see from their windows,
    whether they
    remember us
    our loud
    singing
    and that we were the last ones here.

ANOTHER WAY
March 25

today,
i gave myself permission to be very small
to not jump up and get things when people
mentioned they might like to have them
to not make cheerful comments
or go on any errands armed with my mask and hand gel
instead i sat and played Skip Bo with my boys
didn't do my
writing
softened into the couch
lay on the sand
didn't practice or produce
didn't cook more than a sandwich or an egg
didn't concoct any plans for how we are going to get through this
i sliced a mango and apple chunks and ate them
i let myself be small and soft and a little bit tired,
instead of the very picture of capability.
it is another way to be strong, i think.
another way to be.

WHAT SHE DID
March 26

she woke
and journaled
and worked on some words,
forming sentences she had dreamed about.
she listened, and made lunches.
she walked to the sea and swam. she went on a long walk and collected
tiny shells. her boys grabbed her hands whenever they could. she told her
daughter, "just take a break today. don't worry about school at all."
she made dinner, cleaned up messes, accepted help, coached teenagers in
better dishwashing strategies, absorbed more bad news, helped her parents
book flight tickets. searched and searched for the best way to get them
home.
she kept her cool. didn't take herself too seriously.
she took her vitamins.
she wrote a poem.
she fell into bed,
she fell asleep.
she dreamed.

ASKING AND GIVING
March 27

they came while i was lost in thought—
two beach dogs, possibly related.
my kids name every dog they meet,
especially the ones who come back again and again,
so now the dogs on this beach all have names.
maybe they already did,
maybe because of my kids
they now have more than one name—
tiny assurances that they are seen,
that they are known, that some kids
want to run beside them
or help them catch crabs to eat,
or stand there with them, chatting away.
the two that flopped down next to me today were
Delta Force and Grizzly,
i think.
Grizzly : bigger, male,
a bit more scarred around the muzzle.
Delta Force : sweet and shy,
happy to run ahead of us
pretending she knows the way.
i had been sitting by myself,
thinking about a thousand things that i cannot control.
Delta Force came very close and licked my knee
i scratched her head,
just gently on top
and
when i stopped she put her paw on my hand
and pressed down
again
so i scratched her head,
and every time i stopped,

again
and then her brother came and did the same,
so i scratched his head too
they asked so nicely for what they wanted
again
paws ready, if i stopped scratching,
to let me know what they needed
a thousand things they could not control
but there we were
taking comfort in asking,
and giving.

FALLING IN
March 28

he is made up of so many
particles
his face the complexity of what feels like a hundred years
marriage and children and
memories of loss and
adventure and happy boring hours
light and sleepy mornings,
telling stories, so many meals
songs and smell and skin

that i can't tell what he actually looks like.

i look and it's not like seeing, the way you see something for the first time.
it's more like falling into a well,
or seeing
beyond
seeing in layers.
to me he looks like he did twenty years ago, and like he will in another twenty years. he looks like me, and he looks like our sons. he looks like oceans and birds and music. he looks like unfortunately timed arguments and many, many hugs.
he looks like the feeling of his lips.
i never will know what his appearance is to a stranger, what they see when he walks down the street.
i squint and almost see it,
but then there i go, falling in.

UNSCATHED
March 29

what a mix of feelings this world
offers
one moment the branches of a beach pine
waving in a breeze,
sand under my feet,
the next, stepping on a sharp shell in the water,
gasping, pulling its spike out of my foot,
limping all the next day.
being here with all of it, the tree and the shell,
the loveliness and the ache
seems to be the long lesson.
the trust and the questions
the desire to accept and the need for an apology
contentment and resistance.
i wonder how they exist together
and i know the truth is
if i hadn't been on the beach in the glorious surf,
i wouldn't have stepped on the shell
my foot would have been whole and perfect,
and i wouldn't have limped
my eyes wouldn't have filled with tears
and then i might never have known about the beach,
the softness of the water,
the sand, or the pine,
walking straight,
unscathed because i hadn't experienced any of it
at all.

THREE OWLS
March 30

three owls watched us from the trees
seemingly just as curious about us
as we were about them.
we had been tossed around by the waves
a bit more than usual
putting up with a rough sideways current
because we knew it was our last swim for a while
last blue sky
and when we grew too tired to fight the current
we took a long walk
stepping under a canopy of casuarina trees
there was a
hush
needles thick under our feet
owls watching, swooping silently
branch to branch
curious about the leggy human family wandering
so openly in the forest
so cute, and vertical,
and seemingly unable to fly.

THE DISTANT VIEW
March 31

it is so odd to circle each other
warily
giving space in convenience stores
the lower halves of our faces obscured.
i prefer the distant view from the car--it looks the same as always,
tires humming along on these Thailand roads that have
seen better days
a farmer gliding on a plow in a watery field
children sitting in the shade on the side of the road in
the sleepy
afternoon
the flowering trees lining the highway,
great full blossoms hanging like bunches of grapes
smoke rolling in from the fields as we pass,
windows open,
driving north to the mountains
heading home.

APRIL 2020

ON THE DRIVE HOME
April 1

we
drove past fire,
shared looks,
didn't let the kids out of the car much.
sang at the top of our lungs,
spoke softly and respectfully to officers
who took our temperatures eight or nine times
in two days.
we split the driving
and took turns choosing songs
i snuck looks at your beautiful face,
i couldn't get enough.

WATERING IN THE DRY SEASON
April 2

perhaps i will hike forever
hauling this sprinkler along an acre of land
from the banana trees
to the mulberries
to the cabbage
a good kind of walking
but
it's possible i will do it every day of my life

while mynahs observe from the compost heap
the ants find their chance to bite
and the leaves crunch underfoot
or maybe
i will wake in the night to a long, steady rain
it could be tonight—
or tomorrow
or next week.
it could be.

GOOD THINGS
April 3

    my two youngest sons
    helped me in the garden
    in the smoky late afternoon
    the eerie sky outlining them in light
    as they passed through the sprinkler.
    they competed over who
    could harvest the most
    seed pods
    from the old kale plants:
    i got ten! i got twelve! that one was mine!

    they rode their bikes down steep paths
    laughing when they fell
    and managed to tug a hose until it broke
    while they watered roses

    they remind me of puppies
    they can't seem to move without falling
    over one another
    they are soft
    they bring joy.

    after dinner we made a tick on the wall
    for the second day of quarantine.
    the three of us held hands
    we gave thanks for good things
    for the bikes
    for the garden
    for the seeds
    in my heart was a clear
    fierce gratitude
    for them
    for them
    for them.

TO DO
April 4

      water the banana trees, all of them
      play with your dog
      sit on the grass
      before the ants find you
      eat a
      mango
      plant some seeds,
      maybe rocket and kale and some
      kind
      of flowers
      draw,
      listen to what the kids have to say
      do a load of laundry
      wear a mask for smoke
      don't exercise too hard in this air
      pray for rain
      trust.

EVERYTHING BRIGHT, CLEAR, AND BEAUTIFUL
April 5

it has been all
water around here
dodging sprinklers
checking whether the ground is dry
ordering drinking water
making ice in muffin pans.
and air!
apps and filters, checking the
sky
wading through smog
avoiding particles.

—now it's time for color
for paint and fabric
time to sit in a circle of embroidered scraps and
look at all those colors and textures
go for a stroll among the most brilliant blues, pinks,
vermillion or saffron,
cobalt and turquoise and everything bright
clear
and beautiful.

TO CELEBRATE
April 6

    to celebrate the fact that we could see the moon through the haze
    we lay under the jasmine bush and looked up at the sky.
    we envisioned being stuck to the side of the earth,
    like magnets on a fridge
    and talked about Jupiter's moons, the sheer size of them
    and how our moon is so close to us,
    compared to the moons of other planets

    i love ours, i said, looking at it—
    i could see its marks and texture,
    the rabbit's long ears
    the whole bright friendly face
    i'm glad we get to have it.
    we wouldn't have the life we have without our moon, he told me.
    it stabilizes the earth's path with the sun,
    and shields us from things that might harm us.

    i could picture it then, holding on
    in its particular orbit
    doing God's work by moving slowly
    through space
    being brilliant
    and kind
    and our very own, that's all.

    i'm glad we get to have it,
    i said again
    from my place on the side of the earth, under a jasmine bush,
    looking out at the friendliest rock in the
    whole
    big
    sky.

HOW IT WOULD HAVE APPEARED TO LEAFY
April 7

it would have looked as though his parents knocked briefly,
then burst into his room,
scanning the room wildly.
he had been reading a book,
stretched out on his bed,
a fourteen-year-old in his own space.
he would have seen his dad give the room a look,
shake his head
and say,
"this is no good at all."
"but," his mother would have said, "there are no birds in here."
"there will be! on the mic!" his father would have replied,
and his mother would have sighed and said,
"okay. no good."
and they would have left without saying anything to him,
left him baffled, full of awe at how weird they can be sometimes,
maybe never knowing that they were simply looking for
a place to record a single voice
a quiet place,
without the sound of birds,
a rarity,
and Leafy might never know that it was better for him
that his room didn't suit.

THE DAY'S HEAT
April 8

the pavement in the driveway soaks in the day's heat
so that when you lie back on it
in the dark
you can feel the past,
the sun's rays from hours ago.

too much haze to see the stars
but they would be from the past as well
all the years piled up on each
other
each year skidding into the next.
they are nice to think about
—things that have been here a long time
trees and organisms
earth formations
stones.

nice to think about new things too,
flowers and blades of grass
adult teeth, longer bones, hairstyles,

mornings
with their very present mercies,
always new.

SOMETIMES
April 9

      sometimes it is
      okay
      to simply go to sleep
      after the moon comes up
      (so orange tonight)
      you haven't figured anything out
      proven anything
      you don't have to explain yourself
      or justify what you want
      how you think
      what is inside your heart
      or what you are.
      you don't need to give explanations
      or a thesis, you don't even need to make
      excuses.
      you can just curl up
      in bed,
      let your eyes drift shut
      float
      in the cocoon of being your own self,
      allowed, permitted, and released
      to be.

LIKE A FLAME
April 10

Solomon dances.
it is one trustworthy way to
express himself,
one of the only ways
he can be confident of
saying what he means
because words are slippery
and it can be hard to be heard

but when he dances,
we all stop and look
and we laugh out of sheer happiness,
it's impossible not to.
yesterday it was to the rhythm of my mortar and pestle.
i was smashing garlic
and he came to dance beside me
and my heart lifted,
i smashed garlic longer than
i needed to,
just to be beside him
while he danced.

today, it was the end credits
for the movie we watched.
there had been a thousand or so
misunderstandings throughout the day
a hundred times i asked him to pursue
peace rather than arguments
over things that have no meaning
details no one can prove,
a dozen small storms on this one day
(not unlike other days)

but then the movie we all watched
and the laughter
and then, as Leafy put it, we must have said
his activation word or something,
because he danced like a flame
like a whole stage of dancers
like all the world made sense
like he was made of light.

UNLESS
April 11

      unless a kernel of wheat
      grain of rice
      coriander seed, dried bean, long tree pod—
      seed of any kind, really,
      falls to the ground and dies,
      it can bear no fruit.
      and
      he spoke these words to tell them how he would die
      the dark pocket of earth,
      the way he would go down and down
      curled in around a still heart
      and this only after all that pain
      the unnatural ways our bodies can be broken
      and
      leave her alone, she has done a beautiful thing to me
      she readied the seed for its burial
      deep into the ground
      and what you sow is not the body that is to be, but a bare
      kernel
      not leaves unfurling, or a shot of blue in the grass, not a tree nearly
          as wide as a village
      a tiny shriveled thing really, this seed
      compared to what it will become
      she has done a beautiful thing
      readying the seed for the ground
      it looks dead for some
      time
      sown in weakness
      it feels like we too, are in the ground
      waiting in the dark earth
      unless a kernel of wheat falls
      it looks dead for a long time

she has done a beautiful thing to me
this has been a hard and unforeseen fall
i tell you a mystery
the mortal must put on immortality
he waited there, in the earth
low in the deep place
far down in the place between the falling
and the fruit.

MORE SEEDS TOMORROW
April 12

    i'm not going to lie
    i'm
    a little too driven by my emotions
    sometimes and i was feeling
    lackluster about being in the garden and i know
    it was about the peas i planted they weren't germinating
    and what's the
    use of planting things if they don't grow but
    today i was out there watering something that looked
    like bare dirt and then i saw them the
    first little pea shoots looking like their
    very own selves right off the bat and
    it made me remember earlier we were on zoom with some people
    in my community and my friend who used to be my
    neighbor but is now across the world said that the
    little seedlings have to push so hard on the earth to come up
    they have to push so hard
    and it made her think about resurrection and i
    thought about that and wondered about Jesus in the tomb did he
    have to push so hard to come out
    to get the web of death off of him the packed
    earth off his head which was harder the death or the
    resurrection
    and anyway i'm feeling better about the peas and i'm
    going to plant some more
    seeds tomorrow.

I THINK I AM CHANGING
April 13

tonight the sky has cleared enough so that
we see a smattering of stars,
and when i walk in the dark
around the jasmine-scented garden,
there is so much scuttling
on the ground in the dry leaves.
what is it? i use a light to try to catch it,
but never do. some unseen creature scurries at my
feet while i walk.
a blue headed lizard? a rat?
some nocturnal animal i have never met?
it seems friendly at least.

today was good. Solomon sat in a chair, painting the landscape,
while Leafy and Isaac played a game that involved elastic
 bands and
rocks
and a lot of shrieking.
the neighbors get a concert always,
from Chinua's music room.
(they didn't ask for it, but it comes to them free)
piano, trumpet, guitar, mandolin
you are lucky, i want to tell them, *and i am too.*
we are the only ones hearing this right now.

we sat and discussed world events like scientists.
it is how we do it,
how we have learned to get through things in the past.
yes, this is hard, but how curious, how interesting, how rare.
eventually the emotions will burn us,
we can never keep them away entirely.

i think i am changing,
choosing peace over control.
i still haven't learned not to wish to be more than i am,
however, or how not to long to do more than is
possible for one tall woman,
but there are so many good things and i can't dwell in my own
    failings
i have eyes and ears—i cannot help but see and hear beauty.
maybe the blue headed lizard, the rat, or unnamed nocturnal
    creature

that i can never see

will show me what i am not capable of,
help me to not want to be
more than i am.

FOURTEEN DAYS
April 14

"what will you do?" i asked him
on the second to last day of quarantine.
"what are you looking forward to?"
"i don't really think that way," he said
(he has told me this a hundred times but
i don't believe it—i keep asking)
"but i think i will go to the workshop
and finish building the table saw."

it struck me then—
we will leave this place.
carefully, of course,
going places where we will be alone
but still.
for such a long time now, not one of us has gone away.

what a gift this has been,
what an unexpected, ornery, unsought-for gift.
seven people on one property for fourteen days,
all these ones i love the best.
not once did i wonder where someone was--
if i wanted to know how they were,
i found them and asked.
we ate together every night,
it is a mother's dream,
a certain stage of mother, the one who sees
the beginning of the end of everyone in one place,
as she prepares for the inevitable scattering
it is soothing to the soul, not to dial or text,
will you be home for dinner?

just one day left and my heart has been rearranged,

smoothed out, wafted like clean sheets
when we remade the beds today.
here is the most important thing.
we have found each other again here
in bread and water, garden and song,
in quarantine,
for fourteen days.

YOU
April 15

you have permission to exist
you have it—
even when things are hard,
when people are in need
you get to be you.
you get to walk with your own particular gait
and eat the tomato off the vine,
stand and watch the birds,
be late sometimes,
have grumpy days as well as patient ones.
you can make things without wondering
what anyone else will think about them
you can give as much as you like,
be as strong as you want, without feeling badly
for being strong or good or smart
the same goes for weakness.
you can slam doors,
or sing sweetly,
play an instrument that makes your face look funny,
forget things, or remember them.
you can say, "let me think about it."
(say it! say it!)
or, "that doesn't work for me."
you can dream. you can walk away from an argument
and not hate yourself.
because you,
you have permission to exist.

LOVE IN THE SPACE BETWEEN
April 16

i went out
for the first time in my post-virus
town. i didn't like it
at first, i
couldn't help but feel
offended by the silence,
ropes over storefronts,
tape on the ground,
people looking at me fearfully,
turning sideways to squeak by.
even the cicadas were quiet
for this time of year.
i was not allowed to play with the market baby.
this felt like salt in a wound;
the market baby is everyone's love.
she smiled at me, from across the shop
as i kept my distance

and i snapped back into focus
seeing the empty shapes as presence
rather than absence.
there is love in the way we
give each other room,
love in the tape,
love in the string,
love in the space where masks cover our faces,
love in the hot, empty streets,
love for the market baby.
love for her
grandmother who sits playing with
her smiling granddaughter,
a safe distance away.

SO EASY TO LOVE
April 17

my friend died on this day,
four years ago.
i was a speck in his large life,
a bit of ash in his air,
mostly known for being married
to his best friend
and being so close to his wife.
we loved the same people,
he and i. smiled over them
to one another, rolled eyes, shook our heads
nearly bursting with love
for these two—my husband and his wife—
their brilliance.
i am still angry that i don't have him here
to admire them with me.
look, i want to say, he learned how to play the trumpet.
she pranked me with the best Christmas present,
her music brings us to tears
she is still so lovely, she brings me tea and
we do puzzles while we talk theology,
she is still striding through
the world
so easy to love.

HOME
April 18

i watered the banana trees in the top
corner of the garden today
i walked around with the
hose at noon
counting to sixty with each ring of tough stalks
(sometimes i would count again, just for some extra).
the sun was blazing
it didn't feel friendly
i could feel it tapping on the back of my skull
let me in, it said.
no, i replied, politely.
when i was done,
i lay down in a dark room for a while,
the sun had burned all the fight out of me—
i felt a little woozy, a little sick.
it's how i felt coming back from
shopping in the deserted town,
it's how i feel coming in from the
scorched and weary countryside.
how i feel after many social situations
let me in,
i say to my room,
and the cool, dim light, the bed on the floor,
inside the wooden walls
far from the sun
welcome me home.

YOU WERE THERE
April 19

    i hope all these words cascading on each other
    will distill into a tea
    something like hope
    resilience
    courage
    many times i have felt a different
    infusion— fear
    or despair
    or shame
    and i no longer want to drink from that cup.

    words collect and become stories
    and stories in season call us to
    remember
    we tie them in bunches and hang them
    from the rafters
    we let them cure and become dried and full
    scenting our air with their beauty
    and sorrow.

    your stories are your life
    the path from this day to the next one
    and you are allowed to hold the words in
    your mouth
    taste each one and decide which to keep
    which one goes in the blend
    what you will remember
    and what you will pour down the sink.

    don't let others be the only ones who tell your story,
    they will have their take on it
    but you have your every day.

i hope these words, cascading on each other,
collect into a steaming cup,
one you can drink in the morning
remembering how these days were
and that you were there to see them.

SNAPSHOTS
April 20

the day was an absolutely ordinary one
but with many images that i see now
taking turns to step politely
through my mind

•

Solo on the roof of the car
a hundred poses while my shutter never stops
arms and legs akimbo
face in constant motion

•

Leafy doing push-ups while he waits for sites to load
again
and again
so many push-ups
his face laughing back at me
when i tease him about something or other

•

a spray of water in the sunlight

•

Kenya getting teary over a book she read
when she was a little girl

•

a jackfruit falling from the tree under my knife
rubbing oil on my hands to cut it
chopping this massive thing into pieces

•

driving to town, a mask on every person
who rides by on a motorbike
a drift of clouds
people selling in the market
beautiful with piles of
fruits and vegetables

- Kai slinging an arm over my shoulders
finally admitting how sad he is
to not go back to school

- bread from the oven

- mustard seeds spitting

- my arm over Chinua's ribs

- Isaac's perfect face, the soft skin of his cheek
the way he comes down to the studio in the morning
to climb on my lap

- a lit candle
a flame
the morning prayer in front of me

- my hands

A FLOCK
April 21

in the country where i live
so many of us ride motorbikes
all these cheerful faces every day
nodding and smiling
the virus has changed things
and we are all so cute now
everyone with masks
cloths of different colors
over our noses and mouths
some people with pointy masks look
almost exactly like birds.
we chat in the market
joking in the normal way
our voices are always muffled now
adding new complexities
to speaking a second language
and we really are like a flock of birds
on our bikes
nodding our heads with
extra emphasis
widening our eyes
talking to one another
with muffled, strange calls.

HOW EASY
April 22

how easy it is to want to
know it all
to capture all of it
nail it down, and then
bow a grand bow.
to understand why this happens
or that
where we are going
how to shield ourselves
and how to make it fair.
•
i sit at my small table
with my prayers spilling out of me
eyes closed
and can't absorb what i am trying to do
see the great swirling love of the
three, the Father, Son, and Spirit,
the way they inhabit the universe
without fear or bitterness or strife
simply being in love
like fire, like thunder, like the
earth opening up and swallowing me whole.
how am i supposed to understand,
comprehend, or imagine
that power within me, within my heart
and hands?
•
when i water the trees with the sprinkler,
the birds who live with us see their chance
to play in the drops
they were so hot today
sitting in their trees panting, beaks open

that they all crowded into the spray—
four bulbuls, a dozen sparrows, a magpie robin,
some other small birds—
they played
in the water, ruffling feathers and plumping
up, soggy birds
so delighted, so comforted by
a few drops

•

and there was the grass,
it needed something to drink
and
my son also was thirsty
so i poured a cup of water
and put it in his hands.

INCREDULOUS, HILARIOUS
April 23

the river was dirty today
but we swam in it anyway
and gave thanks.
the sky also, was still polluted
but we could see the mountains
and so we gave thanks,
loud and effusive thanks.
on the way home, we saw the sun set
and then we drove a little farther, past the peak,
and the sun rose again above the mountain,
so we saw it set twice
and we gave thanks,
incredulous, hilarious thanks.

MORE TIME
April 24

i had plans today
and when they were canceled
i was relieved
not because i didn't want to see my friend
(i did)
but because it gave me more time
to lie down on the grass
and think about
what to make
for supper.

MAKING HER ROUNDS
April 25

today when i got to the market stall
the baby wasn't there,
not with her grandmother
or her mother,
or her father.
"she's gone visiting,"
said her grandmother when i asked,
"she's with the pork seller."
and this is how i know
that things are beginning the slow return
to normal
in our small Thai town—
the market baby is making her rounds
for everyone to admire.

PROPHET
April 26

yesterday we found
a baby bird in our house
a fledgling sparrow
injured and lost
my daughter made a nest for him
she has a lot of experience
with baby bird rescues
knows that nothing is certain—
and today
it seemed that his leg was broken
he wouldn't eat
and though he was brave and
feathered
flapping his little wings,
calling for his parents,
he wasn't getting better.

not one sparrow falls

my friend,
after a great trauma
went through a year of
thinking about the sparrow
trying to understand
why they have to fall at all
whether they are really seen
she made the most beautiful art
her sorrow and wrestling
conveyed in lines
and shapes
and prayer—
holy grief

she called the drawings

The Sparrow King

for the suffering Lord
of the fallen sparrow

do you really see?
the whole world grieves.
do you hear?

today, in our kitchen,
my husband prepared a gas
to euthanize a bird too hurt to heal

and my daughter held the brave
feathered baby in her hands and wept
for a bird she had found yesterday
tears sliding down her face
like a prophet, she told us
He knows,
He sees,
He weeps.

ONE YEAR
April 27

we have completed one cycle of
seasons in this house.
we are back to the rainy season,
the freshness of the earth when we first
moved in from across town.
returning to the first season means
familiarity within this space,
we have been here before
and we recognize this form—these shapes
the birds and their lines of flight.
i never think anything will last
and couldn't imagine we would be here
a year later
to see these green trees
the swampy grasses
and otherworldly skies again.
in the same way i stare at my firstborn son
who is almost eighteen.
i remember when i held him in one hand and
six months seemed impossibly distant,
too far in the future to imagine.
when we come back to the
season of smoke and heat in this house
we will recognize it,
and say, "there you are again,"
with happy relief,
the way i recognize each child now.
yes, ten-year-olds are so similar,
six bounces off the walls
thirteen is an old friend.
there you are,
there you are again.

TEA CHOICES
April 28

there was a frog among the tea choices
when i went to get my nighttime cup of tea,
a snail trail a mile long leading to the kitchen,
thousands of winged termites surrounding every light,
and large beetles that landed in my hair
and held on.
there are more geckos than walls,
cicadas in the bamboo,
five species of ant in the house alone
a wealth of crickets and a fresh crop of baby spiders,
and, sigh, mosquitoes.
flies that land on my head in the morning,
Japanese red beetles that eat the garden cabbage
and sparrows in the kitchen, looking for a snack.
should i go on? butterflies on the table,
an owl in the bamboo thicket,
a chorus of frogs in the field past the fence
a hive of bees in the rice barn.
this place is alive,
there are more of them than us,
and so, i took my tea quietly, and left the frog
to browse the selection.

THE RULES
April 29

wrestling and perturbed
the thing is,
i didn't understand the social rules the
first time around
i'm hopeless with these new layers of
complexity
the implication
—sideways glance—
that we are being too
careful
contrasted with my husband's high risk
status
and taking care of all these people
being the connection point
and oh my
i am barely hanging on
and how do you expect me to figure
this out—
but i
breathe in
breathe out
come back to love
and i have sprinkled lavender oil
on my pillow
and morning will come
with the possibility of a better day
but first there is the dark
and sleep
where there is nothing to figure out
at all.

SIX FEET
April 30

six feet is forever.
a distance i cannot cross
but i'm equally terrible with
six inches
six millimeters.
back to it
the confrontation of the gaps in
my intuition
the way i cannot fill in the
blanks.
for a minute there it
felt as though the world
tilted toward the way
i understand it
shifted toward a softer
expectation
six seconds
six days
six breaths
might as well be
six light years.

MAY 2020

YOU CAN COME IN
May 1

coming back from a meltdown
is like coming home
from a faraway place
sometimes it takes many days,
and home feels unfamiliar
after the wilderness outside.
i have to remember
to breathe
to see
Christ with me
loving me as he made me
loving me as i am.
i sit on the steps a while
chin on my hands
birds falling and flying
through the garden
tugging at twigs too big for them
fighting and calling
one gardenia blossom
a drifting cloud.
it's okay, i tell myself,
you can come in
you didn't lose yourself this time either
you didn't fall off the edge.

WHAT WE NEEDED
May 2

the power went out tonight
and inside the house
it was humid and hot
with too many bugs
so we spread a sheet on the grass
and lay there
looking at the sky
moonlit clouds through tree branches
a few stars
and lightning, so much lightning.
Kenya rested her head on my left shoulder,
Isaac on my right
Solomon with his head on my stomach,
Leafy close by
a little squabbling
some singing.
i whispered to Kenya about something
that had happened earlier
i wanted to tell her i understood
and Isaac put his face very close to ours
and said, "secrets? are there secrets?"
we laughed and laughed.
fireflies blinked on and off
the clouds were silver around the edges
sometimes the lightning
made us gasp.
eventually, the power came back on
and we sighed and smiled
went back to dishes
and work
and fooling around in the light

"God knows what we need,"
Solo said, "and sometimes we need to
lie back on a sheet in the grass
and look at the sky."

ONE HUNDRED TIMES
May 3

the humidity was unbelievable
we wiped the sweat off our faces
one hundred times

these strange beetles dive-bombing us.
wearing a mask was a little bit
much
it's all a little bit much
sweaty hugs
sticky hands
and
the most beautiful, shiny faces.

CONFLICT
May 4

things got scrappy around the house today,
in the morning i was distracted by a greater coucal
—a huge black bird with brown wings that look like arms;
we call them arm birds—
skulking by my window,
trying to glide without being seen
like he was on tiptoe,
until he sped up and trotted really fast
to evade seven or eight bulbuls
—no luck, they spotted him and
dove down to peck him repeatedly.
i don't know what their squabble was,
the choicest bits of the compost heap, maybe?
neither do i know about the blue-headed lizards i saw
tussling in a tree
i watched them wrestle
until i heard a thud and realized
one had knocked the other down to the ground.
he took a minute to regain his composure,
then scurried back up, ready for more.
when i got home in the afternoon,
the humans had been fighting
and not even the most frequent offenders.
a punch had been delivered,
wind knocked out.
a younger brother switched off the computer
while homework was being done
more than once.
and at dinner, my beloved said something or other
how dare he?
i drove to 7-11 on the motorbike,
practiced what i would say all the way—

i would really let him have it—
until i remembered that i am
not
a blue-headed lizard or a bulbul
or even a 14-year-old boy
and i
bought my beloved a beer
and took it home to him.

HIGHLIGHT
May 5

    the highlight of today was
    a perfectly ripe mango
    or was it those tomatoes
    falling in slices under the knife?
    or the best moment might have been
    a little pile of olives, cheese, and crackers.
    yes, that.
    or wait, maybe the sautéed zucchini and onions?
    no, no—
    certainly, it was the mango.

THE WORLD OF BIRDS
May 6

under the moon a lapwing
flew back and forth
between the trees and the fence
crying.
i don't know why the sound he makes
paired with the sight of the moon
feels like a long ride on a train
feels like
moving
like possibility.
i tried entering the world of
human opinion today
but it didn't go so well
for now i think
maybe i'll just stick to the world
of birds.

A RISING
May 7

i think about the words
dis-couraged
and en-couraged,
think about beauty
think about strength,
think about courage
and how to renew it:
a long inhale, a setting of the gaze
a flower on the altar
a prayer with each breath
a willingness to be out of control
to make mistakes
to try again. one more hug
one more meal, a long conversation
a straightening of the spine
a quickening of resolve
a surrender, a sinking, a rising
into courage.

POWER OUT
May 8

the power went out at nine
and didn't come back on till five
in the evening.
when it returned
i was under the tree on a bedsheet,
in the heat among the insects
with hardly a breeze
high humidity

the power went out in the morning with
that thwump feeling, when all the electrical objects
stop at once.
i could feel our family giving a collective sigh,
we all knew what this meant—
no work would be done
no fans
no water in the faucets.
we escaped to the river after midday
but the water was surprisingly hot,
even under the bridge
we got in anyway.

"careful of the rebar,"
Chinua said,
and i laughed at our posh surroundings
there under the bridge.
Wookie swam,
proud of herself,
i'm basically a fish, she implied with her eyes
and we nodded politely,
but laughed at her funny wet dog body.
the kids found giant pieces of slate on

the bottom of the river and amused themselves
by writing notes
or drawing with rocks
"you could draw a whole landscape,"
Leafy said. "you could scratch for hours."
an old man fished with a net,
his fish basket over his shoulder.
he scanned the water,
saw us
kept looking for fish.

later, we squelched through the town
nodding to our old neighbors
from a distance.
it was the first time we had been out together
since our quarantine.
we had bubble tea,
sat in our river clothes
and watched the way the world looks now.
quiet, and empty.

when we got home the power was still out
so i spread a sheet under a tree
and lay there with the insects
waiting for it to come back.

BIRTHDAY'S EVE
May 9

the eve
of a birthday
*it's the last night that you will have
a parent in their thirties*
i told them.
Kai stared at me blankly
i don't know why that's notable
and isn't that it?
the way i differ from the rational ones
i think everything is notable
even the ambiguous
even the blades of grass
the turning of the sun
the surprising way they keep growing
and me too
yes, Chinua says, when i find an old photo
and can't help myself,
i have to show him, look how little!
yes, people age
his voice is dry
that's normal, he means
and i know it is silly that i am surprised
again and again by people growing
by the seasons
how is the world so beautiful?
it is just a day, he says
it is just a number
and yet it contains a universe,
i mean to say,
molecules and cells and
cups of coffee
and so many tears and

so much laughter
and all the stupid things i have done
and every meal
and all the stars
and disappointed hopes
and better days
nothing is a number
and everything is a number
and i can barely believe i am still alive
i really couldn't have foreseen it.

SO THIS IS FORTY—
May 10

i check my arms out
they are still there
my one promise to myself this year
is that i will not feed my arms to people
anymore
by which i mean to say
i will not say bad things
about me
or my marriage
or my abilities
in order to make other people feel better

no you may not eat a piece of my arm
not that you asked
i was going to feed it to you
whether you asked or didn't
but
it is okay to be okay
with yourself and myself
so my forty-year-old arms are my own
and i am happy with them.
God gave them to me.
i think i'll keep them.

HUNGRY AGAIN
May 11

last night you spoke of
those first days when we met—
the poem on the stairs the
crazy fun in Washington Square
silly accents
but
today i was thinking of even earlier
the very first time we talked
in the kitchen at the community house
you asked me about Canadian politics
and i made something up
after that we spent so many hours in that kitchen
with others
talking politics and ideas, music and art
you checking the fridge
as though something may have appeared there
since the last time you checked
pouring yourself cereal as the night ticked along
and you were hungry again
so many hours in that kitchen and many others,
loitering,
leaning against countertops,
sitting on tables, talking, talking
i thought of this first meeting
as we stood in our kitchen tonight
with our nearly grown kids
all of you in a
cluster, a clatter of
politics, science, and stories of course
me breaking in with movie quotes
Kai and Kenya pontificating
funny accents

Leafy checking the fridge
you, Solo, and Isaac
pouring yourself cereal
as the night grew later
and you were hungry again.

REVELING
May 12

there are many kinds of luxury
and i like my kind.
perhaps the most luxurious
thing i can do is
take a nap.
you're a lady of leisure,
i tell myself,
after lunch, when i lie on my
mattress on the floor and close my eyes,
drooling on my pillow for twenty minutes
or so,
sinking into a mixture of dreams
and the sounds of shrieks from my sons
downstairs

and then
yesterday, the weather was so hot,
and there were men here
working on electrical repairs
and i wanted to be respectable
until i couldn't take it anymore.
i changed into shorts and a T-shirt
and got into the second-day water
of the inflatable kiddie pool

lying there, in that warm,
grass-strewn water
ignoring the men
looking up at the sky
framed by the green leaves of trees
was the most luxurious moment of my life

and this makes me think that maybe to me
luxury is reveling in something
no matter what anyone else may think.

REMEDY
May 13

it's getting late
i'm feeling fragile and like
i haven't had any noodle stall outings
or long drives
or hugs from friends lately.
i retreat to my room.
it's night now
and i'm lying in the dark
a huge storm earlier cooled the air—
Wookie was afraid of the thunder,
but Kai held her tight
and everyone was good
at the dinner table
and kind
and liked the food
yet still there is a twist inside me
a sense that something is not right.
i try to trace it back
not getting things done
or that angry post i saw
or the other one?
fear that i said the wrong thing
again to a friend?
it could be any number of things
a sharp intake of breath that doesn't
let me rest
as familiar to me as my heartbeat
this rabbit patter
and as well,
the remedy is familiar:
sleep, dear one,
sleep.

HOW I AM
May 14

sometimes i don't know how to answer
the kind words,
"how are you?"
i haven't checked in a while,
or i don't want to.
there is always a pool of sadness
somewhere below
and often it rises up and chokes me
so then i know how to answer
but in the in-between,
in the soft times,
it doesn't feel entirely accurate to just say "good,"
or "well,"
which are the things i might say.
perhaps it would be best to
answer
with news about how fat the geckos are,
in this insect-heavy season,
or to say, warm skin, small hands, and little-boy song
or: i will freak out if one more person screams
or: grass like a carpet, flowing down the hill
cicadas bumping into my lamp
a circle of light in a window
bread making.
that is how i am.

A GREAT LIGHT
May 15

a great light
a great maternal love
has burst forth from my friend,
uncomplex and clear.
she loves this new one:
her paws,
her short legs and barrel tummy
her bat ears.
she loves to love
and —i know because i feel it too—
sometimes love of humans
is like holding your hand out
to a flame
and hoping not to be burned
but in this easy animal love
my friend has the widest lap
the softest eyes.
"It is my favorite part of myself,"
she says,
and
though i love the other parts too
the fire and the pain,
i can see why this one—
this one is her favorite.

IN THE GARDEN
May 16

first Isaac helped me
grumbling over how hard it was
to isolate two tiny lettuce seeds
for each tiny hole.
"how can they make a whole plant?"
he asked.
i agreed with him
it seems it should not be
it seems like powerful magic
"that was fun!" he announced,
and then ran off
forgetting his shoes beside the garden bed.
Leafy was next,
he helped me plant the red oak,
same exclamations over the small seeds
less complaining.
in the next bed over, i planted dill
and coriander
while my fourteen-year-old
middle child kept up a steady chatter
of the spacing and number of holes
and things that came to him there
hands in the dirt
evening sky
nearly night
and we got the lettuce in
but that wasn't the most important thing
that happened in that dusky garden.

ROWAN TREE
May 17

when she opens the car door,
a rush of air comes with her and
a stirring of many long-remembered joys—
we all feel it,
like sunshine, the warmest and
most welcoming.
for me it flows in the shapes and colors of
singing with mud everywhere,
using the mice of our hands,
too many snacks,
candlelight and tea and
six meters of glory,
movie nights and tea, gallons of it,
the way she knows her way around my
kitchen, her dance-off greetings with
my son, her voice over a microphone
gentle and welcoming,
gin and tonic, moving day,
singing in the creek
walking by the canal,
she is in our lives and
was there a time that she
wasn't there?
all the joyful moments seem
infused with her presence
with all the light, all the effusive
tail-wagging, deep goodness
that she carries.

GRAFTING
May 18

before midday,
i went to pick up the raw milk
from a man named Chai.
i've known him for many years now,
i buy milk from him sometimes,
chat with him and his wife sometimes,
responding to
their polite curiosity about me and
my life,
i wave to their baby,
talk about the weather.
today Chai was pruning his lime tree
and i walked through his back wall
to take a look.
he showed me where he had grafted
four different types of mangos
onto one tree.
the avocados hadn't borne fruit yet,
but the coconuts were plentiful.
this language, this language of
trees and starting, grafting,
propagating, has been everywhere lately
and i am watching the man who sells milk
in his element,
watching another friend beaming in her garden,
listening to my father talk about his lavender—
i marvel at the connection of plants
under the same sky,
on different Earth plates
and as i left Chai's home,
waving goodbye, i was

breathing the oxygen that all of this is producing,
drinking the beautiful growth in.

HOPING
May 19

she found me lying on one of the little boy's beds.
i had come up to be with Isaac while he dressed
(he is sometimes afraid of the upstairs)
and though he had clothed himself and gone,
i had not yet gathered the energy to get up.
i lay like a sloth on the mattress and
she plopped down beside me
smelling of mint from brushing her teeth,
and she asked me about sad things from the past.
i told her what i knew.
we talked about how they will all leave one day,
and how i will write a lot when she is gone
so i don't miss her too much
—we both knew this was a fairytale.
we scrolled through photos and
videos of elderly couples with beautiful accents
i can't wait to be old she said.
(oh, how i like her!)
i looked at her luminous skin,
wise, sixteen-year-old eyes, and i smiled.
we will be old ladies together i told her,
hoping it will be so.

THE SHAPE AND BREADTH
May 20

i want angels,
big fiery ones.
i always have.
i want the miracle
a sky shaped being to intervene
in the nick of time,
i want their wings to brush
my face. i want Aurora Borealis
but here in the tropics
and i want it to catch me up,
to lift me so
i don't fall. i want it to bring me
somewhere else, somewhere
quiet yet filled with roaring flame.
i want it all.

i went for a walk this morning
and there were birds, and when i considered
every beautiful thing as love from God
i felt for a moment as though i was
standing under a spigot, wide and gushing.

i soaked it all in, and
who is to say, really,
that the shoulders of the mountains
the hovering clouds
were not the shape and breath
of angels?

SO READY
May 21

Jesus described an upside-down kingdom
where the king is the servant
the servant is honored above all
the least is greatest
the poor widow honored as a great giver
the outsider a neighbor
with great compassion
who takes care of a man near death
the thief the one who will join Jesus in paradise

but you are insisting that victims are criminals
asylum seekers are the killers they are running from
the dead must have somehow
deserved it,
and those who seek justice
are the unjust ones
you say yes those people are dying
but their lifestyle choices need attention
you say the effect
is the cause

these boundaries you are drawing make no sense
chaos is muddying truth
until "the center cannot hold"
we no longer even know our names
where we are from
who our originator is or what God is like

and i think of Jesus in the temple
"He fashioned a whip out of cords"
how long did he sit there fashioning that whip?
knowing he was going to flip those

tables
see all the coins spill, hear that satisfying
rush of clangs, watch people run to pick them up
he must have been
seething
so ready for
the kingdom
to come.

THE FAMILY
May 22

a hen and her chicks have
decided that they like our place
i see them everywhere
every day
in the rose bushes
in the tall grass
in the empty creek bed.
it hasn't rained.
i'm feeling empty, like that
creek bed,
having trouble
remembering that i ever felt full.
it's time to fold back in
to go home, straight home,
right to the place where i can rest.
maybe i made myself a little too
vulnerable?
i am learning not to put myself down
to smooth over an awkward
moment or make someone feel better
but it is a slow lesson
and the tendency is there
the tendency is to run around in the hot sun
calling, *fill this creek bed, i'll do anything.*
today one chick got separated from the flock.
he also stood there
in the creek bed
yelling,
and i could hear his mother clucking to him
from the compost pile
trying to let him know she was there,
but he was squawking too

loudly,
too panicked to hear her.
they love the compost pile,
the very best place to scratch and find bugs.
i snuck up behind the chick to try to get
him moving in the right direction.
he headed, squawking, in one wrong direction
then another
but finally he saw her and sped on his short bird legs,
all the way to where she was.
the rain will come. it will,
the water will come
and i think that it is good that these chickens
like it here.
i am glad it is a good place for them,
safe, and a bit wild,
and full of bugs.

SIDEWAYS
May 23

a new moon circle of women
gentle voices
soft hearts
kind, wise words,
and singing.
it's all a bit too lovely
after a long while,
and belonging is something
i try not to look at head on
best to look it sideways
in little glances.
i made dinner and
needed mangos
for that bright sweetness
in the noodle salad.
at the first fruit stall i found,
i chose each mango carefully
placing them in my bag
and the woman at the shop
began to sing
so i slowed down to hear her
a Lisu song i think
with searching notes.
her daughter was learning
the Thai alphabet and calling
out the letters
loh ling! sho shang!
the mother kept singing
while she took my money
into her hands.
best to look at it sideways
in little glances.

NINETY-TWO PERCENT
May 24

i didn't go anywhere today,
my gift to myself
not even to get groceries
although we could have
used a couple of things
and restrictions have been lifted.
the heat pressed in on us
a large wet hand
until every one of my senses
was pinging
no one could touch me
and if one more ant crawled on me
i was going to explode
these are the less cute
realities of living in a hot country
the senses
how they heighten
how a sound in your ear can make you
crazy
but there are the bananas as an apology
for ninety-two percent humidity
and fireflies,
frogs,
and jasmine. there is jasmine.
so i didn't go anywhere today.

DAILY THINGS
May 25

coffee
pray and light the candle
write in your journal lines and lines and you are here
walk and own the world by looking at it
write a poem
hug and kiss your family
make bread
gather flowers
(you are allowed to enjoy something this much)
drink water
stretch yourself toward a constant, a faithful,
reach for that longed-for, skittish equilibrium,
a leveling of the heart and mind,
don't wait to feel like anything before you do it,
don't overthink it, don't look too hard at it
be here for them
and if you crack, if you dive down hard
if you fall out of the gentle sway of constancy
melting down low and aching like a broken limb
come back, come back slowly
to the safety of daily things.

WAITING
May 26

    we wait for rain again
    the heat is heavy
    sometimes you can see it
    in our eyes
    if one thing is heavy then
    maybe another thing is.
    that's the way it works
    but a sudden wind may come up
    and turn the leaves of the tall
    trees over to their silver undersides
    ripple the grass
    toss the seed pods into the air
    to fall in a shower
    and we feel that too
    we feel blown clean
    and like we could fly.

THE SHAKING
May 27

reaching for something like
clarity. if i find a word
i think clarity will
break open.
if i find a string of words—
ah well, they've all been said.
yes, but not by me.
sometimes people need a friend
to speak the words we all need to hear:
be loved
tell the truth
be free
do better
do not be afraid
it may feel lonely
but you are not alone.

when we are here
in the broken space
where all our assumptions are
cracking open
it may feel like everything is shaking
but God does not leave
the Three dance in
and everything else may
blow away
in a hurricane of severe love
all the fixtures and walls
the way we thought it was
will be gone forever
but God will remain

closer than a brother
dearer, sweeter, kinder,
wings tight around you—
do not be afraid.

RIOT
May 28

i told him
(this was before the burning started)
that i felt like throwing bricks
through windows. just one
or two.

the truth is
my proclivity to rage
is never far away
i get it—I understand the falling in
the way a switch turns and
everyone decides
ah, well, let's just do this next thing
no one cares about us anyway
and i haven't had coffee creamer in ages
i would like a vacuum cleaner
and maybe I'll bust open that safe.

i didn't throw any bricks
(or steal anything).
i painted a portrait of George Floyd.
i kept getting caught up
oh how beautiful
i would think
as i often do while tracing an
eyebrow
a cheekbone
a lip, and for a moment i would forget:
he's gone now
this page has been torn
out of the book

they couldn't be bothered to let him
breathe.

i saw this kid talking
getting emotional,
trying to say no, we didn't want this
we didn't ask for this
you are doing this to us
and i thought, that kid is being
traumatized by this
by these videos
and you know what trauma does to
the body
and brain
and i've heard my brother's stories
of prison, of working the fields for free
in the twenty-first century
and the way the guards would make them fight
set them against each other like dogs

Isaac stood behind me at the computer
while i was scrolling through
and that video started
and i fumbled with the mouse and scrolled
away but then
another one came up and the videos are
everywhere and his beautiful face
is on the ground
and *"don't look!"*
i screamed and Isaac turned away
immediately
not seeing but understanding
from the tone of my voice
that this was not something he should see.

so fires and breaking
oh i know they are not within

the bounds of the law
but the law has failed us

and—i get it—
sometimes burning seems
like the only audible voice
at all.

LOSS
MAY 29

    nothing comes

ABOUT BREATHING
May 30

all that comes out right now
when i try to write
is anger
and when i try to breathe
i can only think of not being able
to breathe
it is the central thought of the last months
this breathing thing
for one reason or another
illness or brutality

the fragility
of beautiful human bodies.

THE LINE DRAWN
May 31

    you didn't watch it, did you?
    i ask my daughter.
    no, she tells me.
    good, i said. please don't.

    how are you doing?
    i ask my son.
    okay, he says, i watched the video— no
    it's okay, Mom, it's okay. i'll be okay.
    i always am.

    are you okay? i ask my husband.
    how are you doing with all of this?
    this is not my first rodeo,
    he tells me.
    he's been through it so many
    times.

    and then there is the little one.
    why is there so much about
    Black Lives Matter? he asks me
    as he visits my writing room
    when he wakes up in the morning.

    all my rhythms of work have crumbled
    i am caught
    and captivated
    and sick.

    because people sometimes need to say it.
    but why now?
    the police have killed someone.

i say.
my son is seven when i tell him this.
a Black person?
yes.
and so they say that Black Lives Matter?
yes.
but everyone knows that!

we know that. but not everyone
knows that.
some people think Black people are bad?

yes.
his eyes instantly fill with tears.

but Daddy is Black! and he's not bad!
i am hugging him as tight as i possibly can.
Black people are very very good
i say
the people who don't think so are wrong
and we know they are wrong.

he looks all over my face. pats my arms.
and you know that. but you're white.
i know it. it's called racism,
i say. it's something we need to fight
it means thinking stupid things about
people because they have a different
skin color.
it started a long time ago. remember
we talked about slavery?
how your great great grandparents were enslaved?
oh, he says. racism.
that's what you are always talking
about at the table—
i didn't know what it was.

his tears are dry now.

he is ready to go play
or maybe for me to make his morning smoothie
he wants to ask me about something else
like when he can watch a show
or whether he can buy a snack
at the corner store today.

we are always talking about it at the table.
now he will know what it is
i feel the line drawn
between then and now.

JUNE 2020

MON ONE JUN
June 1

when they were young,
my children made up a
holiday. two actually.
there is some contention about
who made it up.
i remember it being Leafy
and it seems like something he would do
but Kenya swears it was her
and Kai...
but, i digress
they were called Sun One Jun
and Mon One Jun
(all the words are pronounced
to rhyme with sun)
today is Mon One Jun
(it only comes once every seven years)
a time to celebrate when the first
day of June falls on a monday
and you can say
happy Mon One Jun.
that's all it is.
today they celebrated
Mon One Jun
by eating ice cream
and practicing saying mon one jun backward
until they had it perfect
nujj noho num
what can i tell you about what i feel
for them?
all i can say, really
—and you will have to glean it from this—

is that they celebrate
Mon One Jun.

A BREAK
June 2

the crickets are so loud that
i can hear them in my bedroom
i've been here all day.
sometimes you just need
a break
from
life.

EVERYONE
June 3

i hid away,
like i said,
but not completely
because at different times in
the day
nearly everyone
in my family
came to find me
and for a while, Chinua curled up
beside me
with Isaac in
his arms
and i was so thankful
to rest
and not be alone.

CUTER THAN IS DECENT
June 4

what a thing!
to see friends
and talk about deep
and less deep things
to watch a movie,
eat popcorn
and observe a small black
puppy being
cuter than is decent.
to see all my teens and kids piled
on and around one sofa
in someone else's house
to be friendly,
to be friends,
to laugh.

DISARM
June 5

    what is the best way to talk?
    is it over tea?
    or chocolate?
    cake maybe?
    is it in lines of script
    typeface on a cold screen
    or in emojis
    audio text
    or memes?
    i want to know about logic
    facts
    and argument,
    how to trace the thread
    back to its root
    to disarm
    to listen
    to understand.
    and i want to
    learn how to speak
    softly
    slowly
    over bread and wine.

GOLD
June 6

we said a lot to one another
under the quiet moon
we said a lot
without talking so much
we set up the scope
and peered into it
(sometimes i walk outside
at night and find Leafy looking
through the scope at the stars
it could be any hour
and i love him so much)
the moon was full
and very close
it seemed
every little crater
every ripple
was filled with gold.

Tadpoles
June 7

at our house,
we have many tadpoles.
at first, frogs laid eggs in
a bit of water left in our
inflatable pool
and we left them there
eventually, i said,
i know you love the tadpoles
but i didn't buy that pool for them
we need to find them a new home.
Leafy and Kenya spent a few hours
scooping them all into a large
bucket—
the two of them, they did that.
they set some large stones inside
and a log
for when the tadpoles turn to frogs,
and need a log to sit upon
and sometimes Kenya goes to the bucket
and feeds them bits of papaya
to make sure they are okay.

THE COIN
June 8

i want to be
less afraid of saying
the wrong thing.
if one of my children was
this scared
i would tell them to say
whatever they wanted,
i mean, they know how to be kind
they don't need the precise flavor
or
shade
or adroit touch
of perfection.
Solo likes to sway and dance
on his toes
Leafy to walk in circles
i want them to be free
Kai has his brightness
his fierce ideas
the things
that drive
him crazy
i want to see them free
like the stars
free to be
in their own way
—the disadvantage and advantage
he said
are two sides of the same coin
inextricably linked—
Isaac is like the sun
Kenya cries like me

and then she goes away
and creates
a work
of
art.

BECAUSE
June 9

    i went away
    to edit a book.
    sometime during the second day
    there was a knock on the bedroom
    door of the house
    where i am staying.
    it was Chinua.
    i'm not sure
    but i think he turned up
    just because he missed me.

ON MY KNEES
June 10

i am trying
to be brave
but every day i am
on my knees
first thing
face to the floor
there is so much
in the balance.
how to speak
how to help
what will the future
be
for my children?
what will this teach
them about hope?

BEAUTIFUL NOISE
June 11

after the silence
of a four-day writing retreat
talking to myself,
letting the dishes pile up
because there would only be
a few in the sink at the end of the day,

i drove home in the dark.

they spotted me
they ran to the car
and greeted me with startling noise
a big sweaty group hug
a little dog jumping at my ankles
they were still eating dinner
very late
and

i sat with them,
everyone talking over one another
little digs and jokes,
vying to be heard,
a long explanation
no one had time for

and i was still mostly silent
—a hard habit to break, after
four days—

surrounded by
beautiful

overwhelming
noise.

MANIFESTO
June 12

there will always be sadness
it comes in cycles
and waves
and we are often comforting someone
or cushioning them from the world
when anxiety is too much
or trying to convince
someone that they need to see
bigger
farther
into larger and more potent
justice

so then
(and this is the daydream
that comes in the in-between
spaces of the day)
let's live with as much
wild joy
as possible,
drink it down, play more
than necessary,
do hard things
and be free
allow yourself joy
not just allow,

pour it over your head
in great big handfuls
smooth it into your skin
like lotion
put too much on

rub it in your hair
cook it in your food
add love too
for yourself
and others

throw yourself down
and let love pour into you
from the heart of God

where you are always
a delight.

BESOTTED
June 13

the fact
of your belovedness
can never be taken
away

even if people snap at you
roll their eyes
forget to listen

even if they don't see you
or if it is not your turn to speak

even if you invite someone
for a walk
and they say no
or they don't return your text

or you feel stupid after
you talk to them

if people think less of you
than you deserve—

nothing can take away your
belovedness,

nothing,
nothing,
no nothing

there you are,
God is kissing you

all over your face
humming
like a besotted mother
over
you.

A FEW CONSTANT THINGS
June 14

    the more i am in it
    the more i believe in this
    poetry thing
    the scribbling on sheets of paper:
    do not forget the wasp nest
    or the way the coucal got
    trapped in the bamboo and flew
    away panicking
    do not forget Solo
    and his fierce hugs.
    i have a thousand reminders
    of things i need to do and be
    so it is only proper
    that i also write about the moon,
    my husband's
    lips,
    bodies of water,
    wonder,
    and grief.
    the world is filled with sorrow
    and mundanities
    but there are a few constant things
    hopeful things
    like art,
    God,
    music,
    and poetry.

HIGHER
June 15

    if i can't bear it
    i get on the scooter and
    drive
    even at night
    even in the rain
    let the wind wipe my face
    imagine the bike
    rising higher
    than any mistake.

WHO DO THEY SIDE WITH?
June 16

tonight i
made
rice and tofu
pumpkin seeds and
greens.
we ate, and the
geckos ate bugs and
we talked about how they
are our housemates,
these lizards
who stick to our walls.
there were twelve or so today
finger pads sticking to the paint
catching bugs
watching us eat.
do they know our voices?
are they tired of our stories?
who do they side with in an
argument?
what do they think about
how we do it all?

THE FROGS SANG
June 17

    tonight
    in the humid dark
    while
    my husband played music
    in his tree room
    the frogs—the ones with deep
    croaks that sound like tired cows—
    were singing along.
    each frog had his or her
    own note— held it
    held it again
    held it again—
    in succession, this frog
    song, singing
    along with Chinua.
    in other news
    i paid a fine
    today
    that was unnecessary and
    wouldn't have been required
    with a little
    foresight.
    in every day there seems to
    be a fair helping of
    unpleasant shocks or money
    thrown away,
    but then there are the other moments
    they ones when you truly see the fun
    the risk
    the love of being alive
    like frogs singing in harmony
    in the dark.

SONAL
June 18

my friend, Sonal
—she is everyone's friend,
really— i miss her.
we are on
different continents
in a pandemic.
i think of her in the kitchen
(that is where we often are)
she roasts spices
and tells me
their Gujarati names.
her voice,
her boots,
her animated
friendly scolding,
her face half lit
half in shadow,
the stories of her sorrow,
eating together at the noodle
stall at the Monday market,
there with her dad one day
and mine another.
we have met each other's
mothers
which
in this traveling life
is one of the best
testaments to friendship
two women can have.
we cook together
she raises an eyebrow at me

and my ideas,
remembers Isaac as a tiny boy
comes to sit a while,
slips away quietly.
oh, how i love her.

THE WRESTLING
June 19

enslaved Black people in
1865, two years after emancipation,
were suffering under
a lie built on a lie
built on an endless tower
of lies
we have been swimming
in falsehood
now we
cannot see

God broke Jacob's hip
Jacob the thief who
took what God would have
given him
it changed him—the broken hip
he started to see the way
God sees, i think he
saw that he had
believed the wrong thing

—

one must have while the
other goes without—
this is a lie
one must control while
the other
is subjugated—
this is a lie
a human being more
entitled than another to

breath and life and freedom—
this is a lie.
the lies of blackness and whiteness
and owning and even the false
pretence of equality
wash us
fiery one
change us
the wrestling is due
and maybe,
after the wrestling
after the broken hip
and the blessing
we will see visions
of angels ascending
and descending.

WITH YOU
June 20

>we pulled them down,
>finally,
>the old screens in our kitchen
>covered with years of grime
>bug wings
>and smoke.
>we were all covered in the
>stuff
>but people can wash and
>i was with you,
>i was laughing with you
>and we were getting rid of
>the old screens,
>finally.
>finally.

EACH BIRTH
June 21

he remembers better
than i do
each birth.
i was in the fog and the bliss.
he remembers their different
shades.
Kai was in the caul
Kenya was navy blue
i brought them to me
stunned and
halfway to besotted
he watched us
kissed us
Leafy was quiet
and perfect
Solo was larger
than we would have imagined
he brought us home
he encircled us
father of these five
i leaned on him
Isaac was covered in vernix
and we murmured to him
whispering love
and singing.

SPEND IT
June 22

1. in an world that has
many worlds,
a disintegrated world,
my skin is like a shield

those in power look at me
and don't see a dangerous person
or a criminal
and
though they don't know me,
they keep their guns in
their holsters
their voices friendly.

2. someone i love and i were both
arrested as teenagers
i was carefully shepherded back
to the
right path
while he and his Black skin
confirmed their suspicions
and he was tossed
down a
different
pipeline

this phenomenon is called white privilege
a strange term to describe
a seemingly more palatable
form of hatred

3. the fires of justice are burning

and won't stop
until
every place is level
every human
known as worthy
of gentleness
respect
and restoration
but until then
i think about this privileged skin
i am in

i didn't ask for it
i hate the ugliness of this system
no poetry in it at all
but maybe privilege is like money
if i hold onto it
hoard it
it will corrupt me
it will own me
but
if i spend it
if i open my hands and throw it
in great bucketfuls
if i use it
to be beautiful rabble
to cause holy trouble
to dive into the hope of the scrum

to make a sign
a poem
a life that says
Black Lives Matter
and because they do
we all do
i will be part of the fires of justice.

we can't have some of us

but not all of us
that is not how it works
in God's fierce
creation

4. isn't it the most electrifying thing
when people use
whatever power is in their possession
to change the game
to open the door
to step in the way?

Frodo at Mount Doom
Harriet Tubman going back once more
to set more people free
William Wallace
John Brown
Jesus

i am nt fooling myself
perhaps there is no great need for me
in this world
but i don't want to be
corrupted
i have my life
my love
and my skin

and until the color of my skin
no longer matters
i will endeavor to
spend it.

MAYBE A HERON
June 23

my bones are sore
my teeth ache
my heart pounds like
there is a small child
pacing inside me
wanting answers
that won't come
i will lie on the grass
i will look into the sky
maybe a heron will pass overhead
long and feathered
free of Earth
free of hate.

EFFORT
June 24

today i wrote
in my ideas book
what is friendship?
what are people?
what is a relationship?
these are genuine questions
i don't really get it
what it is i'm supposed to do here.
i spent hours reading
when i was younger
an observer of relationship
in stories
reading how people connected
in story worlds.
i love words
the way they sound and look
the way they meet each other
without any
effort at
all.

EVEN KNOWING
June 25

    in the beginning
    God spoke
    even knowing
    even knowing
    in the beginning
    God laughed
    even knowing
    even knowing
    the long unfurl
    of every flower
    made God smile
    the long petals of
    the first sunsets
    made God weep
    God walking in the garden
    looking for his friends
    in the beginning
    in the beginning
    God said yes
    to all of us
    kissing us one by one
    knowing our shapes
    our fragrances
    and our ways.

THE ZINNIA
June 26

hello, i said,
i love to see you here.
i am a created thing too.
she didn't respond.
she had too many petals
for words,
but i read what she meant
in her colors
and the small places
where the elements had
hurt her.
she was glad to meet me
too
or maybe just
glad to be a zinnia
in a world containing
beauty and pain,
glad to be herself
in shades of salmon, coral, red, and
gold,
glad to be.

HOW SATISFYING
June 27

how satisfying
to buy two kilos of onions
two bunches of cilantro
two bags of sugar
and a large packet of tofu,
to make the beds,
to clip some roses,
to sit with the kids and read a story.
how beautiful to walk all the way
to the river
to get in
to watch my children climb up
onto the rocks
and dry off.

DIFFERENCE
June 28

Elijah McClain
should be alive

should not have died
for being different

i don't know if
he was autistic,
but
he feels so familiar
like a family member
his music
his choice of words
his love for animals

he should not have died
for being free
for being different
for waving his arms
as he was walking home
wearing a mask
walking in
his own
beautiful
way

his mother said he was a healer
she said he healed himself
and others
he gave
and received love

a young man walking home
in a way that suited him

*we will not survive this
if we do not change*

there cannot be
a table or chart for this

if you hold normal where you want it
everything else will feel distant
off-putting
threatening

difference

on an interview
a cop
described Tamir Rice
as a "child in a man's body."
this is some
flimsy justification
for the shots that took his life

no.

*a child in a child's body
a different kind of child's body.*

or,

*a young man walking home
in a way that suited him*

Elijah McClain should be alive
and
if
a boy can live in his own skin

walk on
tiptoe with dancing arms
or in circles
with his head down,
with no threat of violence
if a girl can be taller than
other girls
if people can get along with
animals more than people
if people don't always answer
questions when asked
and that is okay
if some people cover their ears
at loud noises
and that is welcome
if Black boys can rock back and forth
and not be in danger
if people can speak in
different volumes and tones
and be safe

this is how we can all be okay
this is how we can be free
this is how we will be free.

AFTER A WHILE
JUNE 29

okay so
the day started badly enough
face swollen
from crying the night before
rocks in your chest
four and a half hours
of sleep
you've been here before
but you got up
anyway
and you paced
a while
though about pandemics
awakenings
uprisings
and loneliness
after a while
you could no longer stand it
and you went to find him
and you lay down beside him
and he stroked your
hair
the first time in a while
and he kissed you
and you were loved.

SPARK
June 30

God,
clothed in
joy,
walking in the garden
let me join you.
i'm tired.
i don't know what i even
know anymore,
except that i want you.
and all of you,
all the love and the sorrow
all the overwhelming kindness
and anger even.
i want to know the names
of all the birds
and where you see
the greatest hope
today
i want to know what you
see in me
i want to be a spark
from your aliveness.

JULY 2020

HIS OWN DANCE
July 1

last night
Solo played the piano
while we were jamming.
it did not matter that
it was his first time—
he dove into the music
like he dives into water
like he has always
thrown himself into life
rocking around
teeth first
hair flying
singing his own song
dancing his own
kingly
dance.

OUR WAY
July 2

    the delight
    of my life right now
    is how often we sit around
    the table
    talking until late
    till nine-thirty
    or ten
    the dishes waiting
    for someone to scrub them
    while we laugh and shout
    and argue—
    our family way
    of being in love.

PAINTING
July 3

painting, for me
is like a secret desire
the kind of hope
that has been nearly
blown out in a strong wind
—i left it in the yard
far from the house—
but today i pulled out the
brushes and oils
the spirits
the tiny flame of hope
found kindling
as my brushes
burned color across
the canvas.

EXECUTIVE FUNCTION
July 4

something i rarely write
about
at least these days
is how hard i find it to do
normal things, like
clothes shopping
or making plans,
emails or medical appointments.

this is a mother with five kids
telling you this.

so yesterday,
faced with a birthday party
and a pool outing
happening concurrently,
my brain fizzled, burned up,
imploded and then i cried.
i'm used to it.
i figured it out.
sort of.
(i didn't really figure it out
i just worried a lot and
was late for everything.)

i think it's why i like wearing a mask.
i put a mask on and it's like
i'm wearing a grocery shopping outfit.
i imagine myself as
powerful and
wise, making all the good

decisions
about different types of vinegar
or choices of greens.

AT NIGHT
July 5

      he has been so scared
      lately
      and today the fear
      is paired with
      being overtired
      from a sleepover
      and so i lie with him
      as he drifts off to sleep.
      i stroke his hair
      and kiss his face.
      my boy,
      my strong, wiry,
      brilliant
      boy.

WATCHING THE NIGHT SKY
July 6

a few years ago, Chinua
bought a birding scope
so we could see birds in trees
from not so far away

mostly, though,
we use it for
watching the night sky
sometimes i come
outside in the night and find
Leafy using the bird scope
to examine the moon

tonight we saw Saturn and its rings
(shrieks of delight)
the four moons of Jupiter
and the stripes on his surface
through our humble little scope

which is not even made for the sky
but for watching birds in trees
not so far away.

THE WOMEN DANCE
July 7

    the way women dance
    is life, is more than movement
    it is being and heartbeat

    when the work is
    done
    the planting
    or the harvest
    or the cleaning of tin
    walls
    in the slums,
    the schooling, the caring,
    the office job
    when these are
    done

    the drums come out
    the working, leaning,
    bent body is
    thrown off
    (at least for a while)
    and the women dance

    they are more than work,
    more than shelter, more than fire,
    more than home, more than food,
    more than survival

    they move like trees with long limbs,
    they move like birds,
    like created things
    like God's own dear loves
    like the laughing wind.

PETER
July 8

    my friend lost her dad today
    Peter.
    he was like another dad to us, too
    and i don't want it to be true
    —a teacher, a counselor, a
    wise man.
    i remember his expansive heart
    too big for the world
    the way he made us feel like family,
    his laugh, his teasing
    his face when he was joking,
    his prayers.

ENDING
July 9

it has been hard to think
lately,
i find myself standing barefoot
in a room
thinking about death
and ending
and loss
only.
a child running in circles
around me while i
stare out the window
without seeing
unused dishcloth in my hand
stock still
not remembering
where i was going,
why i had the fridge door open
what i came here for
why the scooter keys are in
my hand
where we keep the dog food
what life is
what i came here for.

THE LABYRINTH
July 10

the labyrinth
looked like light
i stepped inside
born
and walking to the center
reliving life
the crunch of each day
the loss of friends
the gain of friends
the children—
there have been many more
than my own—
wedding, ship, dogs with names,
scratched up walls, cockroaches,
more trains than i can count,
eclipses,
tents,
music.
i walked slowly.
when i got to the center
i paused, put the stone
the life,
down
and prepared to leave it.
it may take forty more years
or fifty
or less but
i am on the way out now,
working my way along the path
not only me
but God beside me
like Rilke's poem

walking with me
each day
the green that will come
the sorrow
i am winding my way to the
exit of the labyrinth
this is the second half of the journey
and when i get to the
space where the labyrinth opens
—on what i can't fathom—
i will pause,
take a breath,
and leap.

SATURDAY
July 11

Saturday is the sound of rain
the gathering of sweat
in a power-out
no fans for nine hours
but plenty of talk,
chatting in the hot air
lazily sitting
plucking at guitar strings
sitting in the damp grass
murmuring to our white dog,
holding hands,
with a husband or child
being calm
despite the unexpected,
turning compost
picking roses
and longan fruit
and green beans,
a drive for groceries
being very careful with money,
a movie at home with friends.

PRAYER
July 12

Bright Catcher of Stars
allow me to be
pliable
flexible
yet also strong,
reflective of you
Maker and Lover
seeing the beauty in
each fragile being
approaching
watching
hesitant and reverent
ready to listen,
pray,
exult,
sing over me so i
can sing over others
reaching out softly
standing fiercely
teach me new words
for love
new friendly hope
about the world
infinite mercy
tenderness
and understanding.

WHEN I GO FOR A WALK
JULY 13

when i go for a walk
i feel like i really own the world
like i inhabit it

i put it on like a dress
rather than skimming its surface.
what do i mean by the world?

not Twitter, i don't own that.

i mean that pumpkin vine unfurling
in my garden
a lacy ridge of white
cloud

openbill cranes flying overhead.

opinion finds shallow dirt
plants a seed
may or may not grow,

but these stones are ancient
and that comforts me
when i don't know what to
think
and get confused
about
whether the world will continue
to turn
without me.

HEAVY CLOUDS
July 14

there are heavy clouds
sitting low in the sky
a damp lethargy in the air.
we are all being as brave as can be
and we need more of everything,
more cups of tea,
more colorful pictures,
more kind words
more novels.
we don't know who will still be here
next month.

this is not a small thing,
the not knowing,
and yet,
there is a lot we think we know
but can't possibly,

we imagine our fingers
to be infinitely strong
to hold it all.

we're more like
babies
needing to trust.
more early bedtimes
more naps
more doodling,

a long talk on the phone,
a bit of weeding in the garden,

a good salad.
there are heavy clouds
and we need all the care
we can get.

LAMYAI
July 15

    we climb on top of our
    car
    to reach them,
    the small, globular
    hanging fruit: *lamyai*
    pulling or cutting bunches
    down from the tree
    sitting around the table eating
    one after the other
    —melon, juicy taste—
    or
    merely standing under the tree
    cramming them into our mouths
    tossing the pits
    into the grass
    where new trees will
    attempt to grow.

FLOOD WARNING
July 16

we got the first warning
and discussed
whether we should do anything
about it.
it's hard to pull yourself away
from the cozy light of home
after dark

but flooding,
they said,
from farther up the mountain,
so we peeled ourselves
up from the floor
and went

—or actually, i peeled myself
off the floor,
he put down his trumpet.

now really,
a pandemic is quite enough
to be worrying about
without adding a flood
and also our friends are gone
and money is tight
and our clothes have holes
so a flood would be over the top
really
honestly
but still, we worked,

piling dishes

and table saws
on top of other things
a refrigerator on the countertop
a rice cooker
the mats high up
wood in the rafters,

a table on top of the stove.
we are ready
and so far so good
hopefully the waters
will stay put
inside their banks
we have quite enough
for anyone.

IN THE COCOON
JULY 17

    is it here in the cocoon of
    the lamplight on my bed
    that i find the words to
    smooth the day away?
    snatches of news,
    three conversations,
    prayer and breath and
    waiting —the good part
    untangling conversation
    —the good
    and hard part.
    if i could sing i would do
    that instead
    i would sing and
    sing
    or dance on tall hills
    or at the bottom of the ocean,
    or
    find a way to say
    love love love
    love without clumsiness
    or grief
    love with a true way
    inside
    beyond all the air between
    me and you
    love in this golden
    cocoon.

EVERYTHING BREAKS
JULY 18

in a fit of pique,
the [one] key and the [two] key
have broken on
my keyboard,
which is highly inconvenient
as it also means the exclamation point
(a little too well-used by me
over-compensation for a
propensity for melancholy)
and the [at] sign are done for.
everything breaks.
especially in this climate
the broken strings on rackets attest
the moldering bike spokes
and all of my tea towels,
the line up of household items
ready for repair. i want you
and you
and you, i say.
let's go down to the shops
and look for the person with
the best repair kit
the one who can make
everything right again.
then we will be able to type
[one] and [two] again.
then we will be able to be
exclaim our way out of
melancholy.

WANTING THE OTHER
July 19

and now it comes
i feel stuck.
the stickiness arrived
in the night
like a bat,
swooping and catching
me off-guard.
i was so content!
i was wanting what i had
but now the longing is here
and all i want
is speed
a flight
an ocean
a mountain higher than these
my youth
my country
to be some other creature
anything other than what i am.

WHAT WE SEE
July 20

today i looked through old photographs
of John Lewis
walking across a bridge named
for a KKK member
with his trench coat
and back pack.
possibly he carried water
and medical supplies,
i don't know,
but there were so many photos of him
sitting in,
standing up,
carried out,
mug shots,
congress shots,
holding hands,
marching.
what people we touch
what glorious beings,
full of light,
how can we take it in?
if we could really see them
it might make us fall right over.
it's enough,
—that little defiant smile
"i knew i was on the side of right"—
to change me.

ON A WALK
July 21

a line of coral light
popcorn clouds
silhouettes of trees on a hill
seven openbill cranes
or maybe eight
flying home to their nests.
i stop
and breathe.
this is where i belong.

ANOTHER WAY
July 22

once again
i left myself
it is a kind of abandonment
this leaving,
a rejection

if i was to give advice
i would say,
don't do it,
don't say the unkind things
don't become a magnet for
the swirling grief
don't breathe it all in
don't transform it to self loathing.
there is another way.
i'll tell you

here:
lie close to your heart
like a pearl,
tuck your legs up,
grasp your elbows,
cradle your belly,
breathe.
say, i'm sorry i didn't love you,
say,
i'll never let you go.

DON'T WAIT
July 23

 is it us?
 are we the ones who will take this
 and change it
 heal it?
 bring a light,
 bring it now—don't wait
 shine it into the hidden places
 don't wait.
 no human is a monster
 but humans working together
 can weave monstrous traps
 machines even they cannot
 take down except
 bolt by bolt
 .

 shake yourself.
 .

 here are some questions:
 why?
 why now?
 what are they asking for?
 can we change it?
 are there enough of us?
 why gas?
 why tanks?
 why camouflage?
 why are we used to this?
 how have we become used to this?
 are we the ones?
 .

 read it again.
 read David and Goliath.

read Jesus
heart and blood and words
read
Isaiah.
.
start new.
talk less
ask for a new way
a way lined with flowers
there are many out here
who have put
their hands
in his wounds,
in his hands
and his sides.
they have wisdom to share.

YOU WERE THERE
July 24

there i was
and i was spinning
dress flaring out
hair turning as i turned
letting the breeze
reach my neck,
and you were there
you were spinning too
i danced by myself
with you
no one could see me
it was a secret
i was so heartbroken
but there we were
and the music cradled me
and your heart revived me
i was spinning
and you were there
you were spinning too.

GOLD-TIPPED
July 25

after we swam
and talked, and ate fruit,
we drove home.
two teens, an almost
twelve-year-old, a
seven year old with missing
front teeth,
and me.
how many times did we exclaim
over the sunset?
this time there were gold-tipped
clouds and so much red light
and the hills in front of it all
and when we got close to home
we couldn't help it,
we turned the wrong way to see
more of the sky,
to soak it in as long as we could.

WAYS TO BE LIFTED
July 26

it's always the sky, lately.
falling stars,
lightning bugs,
a new appreciation for the moon.
the whole family staring at a
comet that won't be around
forever.
three pairs of binoculars.
"have you heard the latest about
the stars?" my husband asks his friend.
they dig in like old gossips,
eager to share.
we all find our ways to be lifted
from the banality and the firestorm.
for some of us,
quite literally,
it is the sky.

WHAT WE CAN HAVE
July 27

let's be honest,
we miss everyone like crazy,
miss the big circles,
the piles of people,
barely being able to walk
without stepping on someone,
food and chai and dessert.
life.
but okay,
we can't have that now.
so we take courage,
great inhales of goodness,
from a drive through the mountains
in the back of a truck,
from giving some few paltry
things away, from love
and kindness, we take
strength from being together,
as diminished as we are.

OVER THE BRIDGE ONE LAST TIME
July 28

when John Lewis was a baby,
his mother held him,
i think, and maybe she tucked
his head under her chin,
maybe she smoothed lotion
into his precious, soft skin,
in the velvety darkness of evening
on a warm night.

i think they looked into
each other's eyes, mother and baby,
that gaze of pure, mutual love.

i hope she never saw
the batons hitting his body,
the sharp cracks,
the disdain and contempt,
the bruises and blood.
the way others dared to put their
hands on him, the violence—

oh, she probably saw,
she lived to be eighty-nine,
and there were photos,
and he never stopped putting
his body in the way.

did the pride she felt in her son
cover her pain?
did it take away her bad dreams,
heal her mind's eye?

it is only fair,
if she saw him beaten,
that she also saw the
way they carried his body over the bridge
one last time, gently, slowly,
a horse-drawn casket
on a carpet of rose petals—
the deepest red—
and she recognized
her baby,
she saw those moments
when she held his unscarred body
and the way the bridge
and the world
held him tenderly again.

STATIONARY STORE
July 29

i am allowed back into the store.
it has always been one of my favorites
and it was a little sad
to stop outside the entrance
and tell them what i wanted.
stationary stores, art stores.
maybe some people feel this way about
jewelry, or tech—as though everything
on these shelves opens a door,
makes a world possible.
i don't know how other people feel
about clothing and shoes, or handbags
but if it is anything like how i feel about
a new pen, i can understand, i guess,
why shopping malls exist.
paper, notebooks, fineliners, paint.
i have to remember that it is the
lines that flow that will create
possibility,
which is to say, it is me.
still, it was nice to walk through the store
browsing the shelves,
choosing between paint colors,
looking at different widths of tape.

I WAITED A LITTLE LONGER
July 30

i waited a little longer
so she could ride with me—
if you can call frantic packing waiting.
she needed the stamp that would tell her
that she can continue to live here.
aren't we all so vulnerable now?
to the lines of borders, governments, germs, lack of love,
a long stretch into another person's life?
i was happy to wait.
they gave her the stamp.
we have another year
and we are still waiting for our other friends
contenting ourselves with the garden
and the rain
and the drive down the mountain,
an unexpected twisty ride
through a beautiful day
with a friend.

A SINGLE DAY
JULY 31

i read that we could
unpack a single day
for the rest of our lives,
that is how rich our experiences are,
though we miss seeing so many of them.
a poem does a lot of unpacking.
for example:
waking up disoriented,
in a hotel room, wondering if my
reading was okay the night before.
agreeing to meet friends for breakfast.
their lovely sleepy faces.
rifling through second hand clothes
ordering coffee
exclaiming over
the sparkly velour pants
glittery shoes, and animal-print tights
that my friends are buying.
bitter greens and toast.
a long walk in the sun,
sweaty forehead, long talks,
more talking,
a goodbye at the bus station,
shopping for apples
and cheese,
driving back to the hotel,
writing and writing,
finding myself alone,
saying *hello, how are you,*
i haven't met you in awhile.

these are only a few—
the writer is correct,
i could spend years with that
one day.

AUGUST 2020

JUST WET ENOUGH
August 1

in some places, August
is hot with a scorching blaze that
sucks moisture right out
of your mouth.
some places feel the aching bites of
mosquitoes
the way we do,
or the blast of
heat like a shower door opened,
wet and gathering in droplets.
some places are cold,
even snowy.
and some are like this place,
unfailingly beautiful with skies
reflected in rice paddies
and clouds dipped in gold,
green everywhere, green song
and life and things growing
so fast you can see them
moving.
then the other side,
the rains rushing in
the mountain creeks gathering dirt and sticks
roads turning to streams
so that we check the river level daily,
calling with upstream news,
remembering past floods,
hoping that this year
we will get just wet enough
and no wetter.

A WALK AFTER SILENCE
August 2

    this deep silence is like
    a blanket around me.

    i'm not sure why i call it silence
    —i have the music on—
    but i feel the silence around my
    thoughts, the lack of need to detangle;
    there is no gaze on me.

    i leave the small rented room and
    take a walk, talk to people
    i make two new friends,
    three, if you include the pomeranian
    named Oh Oh!
    everyone always wants to know
    how long we have lived here
    eight years, i tell them
    it is still surprising to me
    a fact that will never not be a mixture
    of happiness and loss.

    the friendliness of the couple warms me,
    they sit outside and fix
    clothes, all day, every day
    or she does, i think he takes the orders
    and runs the business

    they speak a mixture of Thai and English to me
    Thai on its own would be easier to understand
    but i don't say that.

    the dog is afraid of my hat

so i take it off and pet him
he's surprisingly docile
after all that barking

the city gives a lot of moments
like these, and i am full of light
as i walk back to
my silence.

IN THE CITY
August 3

bright lights
escalators
i check in and out
of every shop
wear a mask
hold out my hands for
sanitizer. think—
maybe today the clothes
will be affordable.
no. but we buy
notebooks and pencils
for a new school year
drink coffee
giggle in the supermarket
the teenagers
don't know how to
navigate big stores like these.
they laugh because i have
a cart with only one thing
in it. i put more in, but
take it out
put it back on the shelf.
buzzing brain
time to go
home is outdoor markets
a small shop
and the garden
where i can pick green beans
from the vine.

WE HOLD TIGHT
August 4

i am more with you
than anyone else
thinking your name
seeing your face
even from miles away, i
hear you.

you would love this shirt
but not this restaurant
you would want
bingsu, you would make
us all laugh
so hard in the car.

you would be singing
while it rained, you would
be in the middle of all
of it, your eyes would
glint at me here, you
would notice the statues
of horses. you would eat
salad. i am alone here but
our air is the same air
we are so different
you and i, but we meet
we meet, and we
hold tight.

FIRST FLOOD
August 5

      our community space,
      has had its first flood
      of the season.
      there might be more,
      could be, it's only early
      August, but
      i refuse to
      i will not
      i'm not going to
      i'm far from
      i won't
      i shan't
      i refuse to
      let it bring
      me down.
      there are only
      so many downtrail
      slippery falls, muddy
      tumbles, rockslide,
      low-moan, bedlam,
      ski-slide, motorcade,
      white knuckle, tummy-skid,
      waterplaster, hairtrigger,
      mountain bend, cliff jumping
      wipeouts
      you can take in one year,
      after all.

DAUGHTER
August 6

she comes to me for
hugs
when she is happy
or when she needs to
remember
who she is
and that she is loved.
she tells me things
if i wait long
enough
in the quiet—only then
a shimmer of privacy
her thoughts, her ideas
are guarded. she knows how
give them their full ripening.
she is quiet in the car
sick to her stomach
head leaning on the windowsill
looking out, singing quietly.
i remember that when she was small
she would suck the two middle fingers on
her left hand, and the other hand
would rub my arm, play with my hair
or stroke my face
tenderly.

ARRIVING LATE
August 7

arriving late for meditation
i sit quietly,
but they still notice me coming,
they tell me they are happy
silently—the grass and palms and
bamboo are happy too.

WAKING LATE
August 8

    Saturday is waking late, well, after seven,
    drinking coffee while wandering in the garden,
    shopping for groceries, eating noodles,
    going for a walk, listening to a podcast,
    having many plans to get things done
    but getting none of them done,
    sitting with my dear one
    watching the Mandalorian
    with my head resting on his arm.

RICE PLANTING
August 9

the landlords didn't tell me they were coming.
they never do, and that is okay,
that is the way we have
done things for the last eight years,
it is the way things are
and i accept it.
they came for the second rice planting today
and i would have liked to know because
i would have cleared my day
but maybe this was better,
i had two friends over, Sue and Janet,
from Chiang Mai.
though they have both lived in this country
for many, many years,
neither of them had planted
rice before, and eagerly they traipsed out
to the muddy rice fields with me.
nobody fell, and this was good—Janet is over eighty.
Sue got into the paddy with me and planted a few
stalks. i planted stalks deep in the mud for
as long as i could
and then
it was time to take my guests home,
but i could have gone on forever.

AN OLD STORY
August 10

the rice in this country
has an old story
the roots go deep into
water and earth
will i ever know the story?
the old song
wind in ripples
a cycle of seasons
the planters laugh at me—
my painstaking attempts to
form straight rows
and i am reading my—what is
that word? when there are two
of you and one is not needed?
redundancy, that's it—
i am reading my redundancy in
their laughter
which is kind and
dear God, what have you done?
bringing me here from my country
of apples, wheat and wine
here everything is water,
reflecting the natural lines and grids,
the curving rows of rice plants
containers mud walls
two skies
two worlds
rice above and below
i am hungry busy empty
and the rice is so beautiful
my redundancy

hands in the mud
two of me
are here.

THE CONVERSATION
August 11

the conversation went on,
not face to face but in comment boxes
and long rows of text. i knew it would be
hard to get through. i didn't count on
how often my breath would catch because
of old memories.
we drove down America's highways in RVs
and vans, those old roads, gray beneath
the wheels, cracks fixed with tar
that got hot in the sun.
we were young and barely sheltered
from the outside, at any moment we might not
be able to make our ridiculous rent.
he was more my husband's friend.
she was my friend.
he was nearly a stranger.
we all lived together
i thought we were pressing against the same
walls, the same monster together but
maybe i got it wrong.
Florida was so hot.
in Alabama he told my husband to stay in the RV,
for safety.
Chinua got out anyway,
and i was still barely aware of the danger.
there were more than just alligators in the swamps.

THE LINES REACH OUT
August 12

today i know
nothing
not anything, not
how to get up or
rest, how to pray
or feed myself,
i don't know how to
talk or be in the garden
or enjoy
(i feel like i used to
know how to enjoy)
i don't know what people
are made of or how to
discuss or how to dress
i am face to face with
the sky and the world
my own
life and the lives all
around me and i don't know
how to count them
how to do this next part
how to mother
how to gather courage
how to send and release
but the tendrils of a poem
reach out
to me, the familiar lines
of words
the sound of the river
i can imagine boats there
in the inky darkness

the tenderness of night
and all the unseen
unknown
loves.

FAR AWAY US
August 13

in a pandemic
it is so sweet to have a
simple kitchen conversation,
to tell one another
ideas
and try to fix the problems
of the whole
world. to pretend it is us
maybe we know the solutions
if they would only
listen to teeny
tiny, wobbly,
far away
us.

THE WAY WE THOUGHT THINGS WOULD BE
August 14

it is a low time
it comes around, and
you can't click your fingers and
tell it to leave. a quiet moan
a single hiss, staring at the coffee
not seeing it. maybe too much
came over all of us and we
didn't know what was next.
some of us
laugh it off, some are angry
some can't quite comprehend
it takes us months to process
the litter of lost things
the way we thought things would be
the way they are.

USE FRIENDLY WORDS
August 15

we sat and talked about the self
does it exist?
i think so. i have always thought so
although i have also had a hard time
orienting myself
in myself.

what is it? she wants to know, at least
i think she wants to know.
lately it helps me to think of it as my home
my hearth. my place to sit.
in the low times,
though i have a constant distressing hum
a thread of self wanting to jump ship
it is hard to imagine hating this home.
so i don't.

i open the windows, sing
think of the days, the stories i can tell
sit at my hearth, use friendly words
ask God to come and sit beside me there.
we have so much to talk about.

THESE THINGS
August 16

i scrambled eggs and it was love,
folded in cheese, let the dough for
the cinnamon rolls rise
i made chopped onions to make salsa
marinated hot peppers in lime juice
from the limes on my tree
it was love. i mashed avocado,
made bread
we ate. it was love. cinnamon,
sugar, soft and warm, love
—these days, the lists and ways i know i am
forgetting something, some important thing
that we will discover
they needed
and did not quite have,
i have forgotten too much, there are parts
of this job that i misplace like car keys or glasses—
but some things, this food,
these birthday breakfasts that turn into lunch,
the hugs and the fragrance of dough baking,
these things are love.

A MAN ON A MOTORBIKE
August 17

an older man on an old motorbike
he has cinched shorts,
yellow plastic shoes, maybe a
woven shirt
or a button up. gray hair.
at his waist, a machete
in a bamboo sheath,
tucked into a woven belt
a small fringed bag slung sideways
over his shoulder
brown spatters on his back from muddy trails,
he remembers when many of the roads here
were dirt, impassible in this season
he is going home from the rice fields,
he is ready for food, a dream
a cold drink, a hammock
he knows this season and the
next
all the skies in between,
the memories of his father.

NOTES TO SELF
August 18

1. get up before the sun and go swiftly into the kitchen, turn on the light swinging overhead, make your coffee, inhale deeply

2. make bread

3. do what you do, do your work, listen to your children, do small things

4. the chickens think they know what's up- they think they live at your house. they do not.

5. none of this is the end of the world.

6. it is not the end of the world.

7. it is not.

8. pick roses

9. make sure you get a nap in

10. Isaac has lots to say. listen to him. his voice will deepen and he will say less

11. dream big, big, big, so big.

WHAT WE DIDN'T KNOW
August 19

      twelve years ago Solomon was born
      during the monsoon
      in India, great, gusting sheets of rain
      slamming against the windows.
      i didn't know if i would make it through.
      i had never experienced anything like it
      and had no reference for
      rain that didn't so much fall as
      invade

      i had no reference
      for giving birth in another country
      i never even considered not
      being
      able to do it,
      i didn't know how to measure such things
      and so, i did it.

      i remember that once he was
      born i wasn't as hot
      all the time. that his head was always a little sweaty,
      that we all loved him
      that our neighbor always called him King Solomon and
      that i couldn't find clothes for him
      he wore cloth diapers and cotton singlets
      that tied at the shoulders,
      maybe for the first six months of his life
      it is hard to imagine now, he is so tall and lanky
      and we have so much more experience
      we know more places to find things,
      we know we will make it through.

PLACES WE'VE LIVED
August 20

over chocolate cake and
dandelion tea, we told each other
stories of our childhoods.
Fiona grew up on a small island
in China, moved to a bigger city,
and then, suddenly, startlingly
to Illinois, Arkansas, and then Oklahoma.
she banded together with a girl from
Hong Kong, and one from Korea
three Asian girls in a whole big school,
she eventually learned English
she learned to be from somewhere else.
they were kind, she said, *they helped me.*
Kenya told us about growing up in Goa
and the way our family traveled. Joanna told us of
standing in the hallway in the Philippines
arms spread, books on her wrists, for
forty-five minutes or so. of talking too much
and having to chew on a chili
and i mostly listened and asked questions,
i told of my schools and
being young and learning that normal was relative
and of the way this place feels like home.

THE RAIN
August 21

the rain did not let up
i dreamed awake in meditation
of water carrying seeds and flowing
down mountains, carving paths,
forming seas, dropping off
the edges of our own grass roof
and all the while it rained.
the grasses became swampy and we sank
to our ankles, we splashed along pavement
we carried ourselves in the movement of
water and the rain did not let up.
it did not let up.

DRIVING IN THE MOUNTAINS
August 22

the clusters of bamboo were so dark against
the hills, held close by clouds
and the boulders were scattered like pebbles
—you could almost imagine a giant hand
carelessly sowing them.
i drove my motorbike for a long time.
on one section of road, the corn stalks rose high
on either side, higher than my head,
on another, a rubber tree orchard
waved in my peripheral vision
light winking through the long, thin trunks
a woman walked with two dogs following her
her black hair tied back in a loose ponytail,
the light brown face of another woman showed up
pale against the dark wood of her house,
she sat looking through her glassless window
there were flowers, large orange star shapes
and purple bells
i drove through mud, it spattered my legs and skirt
though i did not fall,
and everywhere— the mountains, the cool air
and the threat of rain.
i was alone, but i did not feel lonely.

THE WHOLE WORLD
August 23

for Solomon's birthday
we had a scavenger hunt
with many clues.
things to find
things to solve,
things to purchase
or ask for. it was chaos
and fun, and the kids—
preteens and teens—
sometimes needed to be wrangled
to be called back to the present
to the task at hand,
i could see them roaming in their minds
see the moment they snapped back into
focus, their eyes meeting mine
alive and full of joy
full of so much joy
and then, before i gave them the next
instruction, they were already heading out
to find the whole entire world.

FAMILY AT THE CLINIC
August 24

sometimes i really see
just how much we like each other—
he didn't leave the doctor's waiting room
even though only one parent was needed
it was nothing serious,
an infection in one child,
sore feet in another
and me, needing blood work
so we sat and talked on the wooden bench
i practiced my Thai reading and he
told me about a podcast he has been
listening to and when the time came
he took the twelve-year-old and left.
i had my blood drawn, and Kenya
had acupuncture—a family day at the clinic.
we lay side by side on the narrow cot
and i showed her silly videos on my phone
to help her through the strange experience
of feet full of poky things.
after she was done and the needles were out,
we went to a café,
and ate cake.

FEELS LIKE BLASPHEMY
August 25

this is a prose poem no beauty here
only a brittle broken crime
i wonder have you ever tried to stop a fight?
i have. i jumped off my motorbike and
got in between a man and a woman
he was hitting her and she was hitting him back
i shook my head about it later, imagine it, me and my skinny arms
spread out between them, shouting 'stop it now'
today i keep imagining what would have happened
if a cop came and shot me in the back
seven times. of course that would never happen
i have this currency called whiteness
my body is not in that kind of danger

have you ever been a bystander
when the cops were called for a domestic disturbance?
we have, my family, all seven of us and they ran in locked and
    loaded
it wasn't till later that i felt like i would faint, when
we realized how dangerous it was
how we were in the wrong place at the wrong time and
we could have lost everything
right there in front of us
all the of kids there
the guns trained on my love, my husband
someone unrelated to the incident
the only Black man they saw
for those few seconds
we didn't know anything about what was happening
we were just there
he was just him right then
naked hands raised, unarmed, unprepared

and that's it, isn't it? just him, and my boys are just
themselves and my nephews are just themselves and
Black people everywhere walk through the world in their bodies
    knowing
that this could be the day their loved ones die or are maimed
the day their children realize they can never again trust
and they were only going to the playground like anyone else
they would, like anyone else, like to visit a friend
not knowing it is the end of something now
or maybe not, maybe this time the bystanders walked away
the suspects weren't executed, or many he will never walk again

and somewhere over coffee and muffins, a group of people will talk
about whether or not there was a warrant
whether or not he was walking in the wrong direction
whether or not he did everything perfectly on this specific day
whether or not he deserved to stay whole.
and you know right this minute
somewhere a white man is yelling in a cop's face
screaming and pulling away and the cop removes his hands and
    lets him
go.

tell me again how we should protest this
how peacefully people should walk, like MLK
tell me again that King was good, palatable, that he
didn't die a violent death at the hands of the system he protested
or Jesus, how he was good, palatable, didn't die a violent death
and actually, it has been peaceful, there have been families
    walking,
people writing books, studying for years, making movies pulling
    out cell phones
it seems it takes a lot to stop them from shooting Black men in
    the back
or Black women in their homes
maybe it just takes fire, tell us how to stop it
maybe it's an eye for an eye a building for a life
a city for a life, no? but

it wasn't yours to take, this life didn't belong to you
it belonged to God, it was never yours, this life was a created being
a holy walking seed of potential, full of unbloomed plants and
days ahead of walking in the sun, of possibility and wholeness
and a life with an unbroken body and the kids who
wanted to run with their dad, and going on as though everything
is the same feels like death, a world without fire would feel like
blasphemy.

SLOWLY WE LET THEM GO
August 26

i was in the air
the air was all around me
i walked sluggishly
as though through water
i made my way to the standing pools
the fish in their places
neither here nor there
moving always from one place
to the next
you could call them always
in motion but that
would not be my name.
i got to the bike
and to the other end of the valley
i lay on the floor,
the coolness of the concrete
like an ocean under my cheek.
i was in the air.
you were there too.
we spoke of trees,
there were too many painful things
but slowly we let them go.

COME QUICKLY
August 27

this feels an awful lot like death, Jesus
can you make your way here quickly?
through the crowds, pause if you need to
when people need healing,
take the time
you know the right time
but then please come,
please sit down,
please call us back, tell us it's time to come back.
reach right down into the darkest place
down and down,
say, *honey, it's time to wake up.*

OUR ROOTS
August 28

a psalm of lament
meditation on longing
the bamboo whispering
against the grass roof
birds in the distance,
calling one another
with news of the neighborhood
these friends i want to love well
Paul praying for us daily
even now, through eternity
that our roots would go deep
straight into love,
hard things, hard things
we can grow taller, resilient in fire
our roots going down for miles.

HIS OWN TERMS
August 29

there is a universal agreement
that Chadwick Boseman
was an undeniably good person
and again, it feels that the world cannot
afford the loss of a good man. my kids loved
Black Panther
and i loved the way T'Challa came
through the portal flanked by sisters—
he always brought someone with him
and it seems unbearably beautiful and sad
that this good man lived his life,
sickness, and death
on his own terms, even now,
on his own terms.

ON MY MOTHER'S BIRTHDAY
August 30

i think of my mother in sunshine
when she was a girl, on this day,
her birthday. what birds did she hear,
did she go to the lake? did she hug her
own mother?
there she is on the porch under the trees
i see her dreaming, what plants did she love?
did she eat cake?
which branches met over her head?
what was her favorite pen?
her favorite pair of jeans?
i have seen photographs, have seen
her smile, have heard her voice in my ear
many times but never then,
when i was not even a dream,
maybe just a far off possible thing
and she swam in the cold lakes
and lay on rocks and listened to the water
flow.

THE NEIGHBOR'S CHICKENS
August 31

the chickens have grown up
in our compost heap. they still travel
together, a flock of siblings,
they come from next door, just after
dawn each day, running headlong,
unwilling to let the choicest grubs
go to the greedy mynahs.
today, just before they arrived, i saw
my magpie robin friend—it's been a
while, but he's back
tail flapping as he perched on the
post. then the chickens came.
you can't help laughing, they
act like big kids, unsure of their
wingspans, what to do with all this
body, their long weedy breed
more like dinosaurs than anything.
hi dinos, we say, as they go cackling
across the yard
the landlords try to shoo them
but i doubt they'll ever leave.

SEPTEMBER 2020

KAI
September 1

       you came out in the caul
       (good luck, the midwife said,
       or the sign of a sailor)
       your father saw you first,
       little spaceman
       you drenched them
       their faces wet with your
       wild entry on the high seas
       as though you danced bravely
       into the room. you were the first.
       we saw you.
       we heard you and everything shifted.
       that was all. marvelous one,
       hair on your cheeks and forehead,
       small face scrunched against the light
       you slept between us
       you smelled of heaven
       we had stained hands
       from the blackberries we ate
       you were our first important story
       the one we meditated on before the others
       what does this mean? all the new smells
       tiny clothes, milky mouth, fists tight
       against the world's end
       and the beginning of something
       the beginning of you
       and love so big we couldn't have fathomed it.

DAYDREAM
September 2

it was a memory of light
of motion, of sun through trees
and the sound of the tracks
thudding under our feet
the way the tea callers hurl their voices
the questionable choices of sandwich.
i lost it,
or it is not reachable now
but you are, and in your eyes
all those memories, you and i and
the train, the white birds lifting off
from temples or buildings
or brilliant green fields.

THAT OTHER HOME
September 3

another day of longing
this one for the clear water in the photos
—if i didn't know the exact smell and taste
of that air, of the sun-warmed skin of children
on the beach, of the exhaustion from the wind
and the blisters from paddles
i wouldn't long so much
for the forested coastline
all that driftwood,
the bright clarity of that other sky
the cries of gulls in that other home.

THE SAFE SPACE
September 4

    the light breeze in the palms
    wet face from crying
    —delight yourself in the Lord
    He will come to help you—
    this is the only safe space for me
    here with the palm shadows dancing in light
    red floor and visiting butterflies
    heart full of grief
    and love.

OTHER THINGS ARE TRUE
September 5

i woke up crying again.
i am tired of writing it
but it is true
and without truth
i cease to exist
other things are true:
real arms and legs
the morning light on the mountains
the magpie robin
coming to say good morning
day after day.
truer than true.

BACK AT SHEKINA GARDEN
September 6

on Sunday i came back to the garden
washed every bowl
put them in the sun, sang little songs
under my breath.
i remember this, i do, i remember
the sun falling this way, i remember
the light, chopping vegetables,
washing and drying, the scent of
spices frying. and then people
arrived and we greeted them
and stood to sing thanks—

half a year has gone missing
we want our friends
nothing is the same.
and yet, we go on,
community lunch, these small comforts
giving food and receiving
washing dishes in the shallow wide bowls in
the grass, passing the talking stick and
sharing names and stories, meeting a
traveler from a place called
Transnistria, a place i have never heard
of before, our little white dog
curling up beside strangers,
these small beautiful things
are the same.

MY STORY
September 7

i remember light. flashes of
movement, the sunrise.
you were there, too.
a break in the trees,
you were there. life in
the water, i danced on a rooftop.

i miss my younger self so much
sometimes, like she is my
daughter. i want to comfort her.

i remember eating momos on
a doorstep somewhere, sitting
at feet level. all those ankles going
by, people pausing to look at me
i remember drinking cups of tea.
the lake in all its light
seeing a water buffalo for the first time
there was so much i didn't know
so many times i reached out
and stumbled but what faith
to reach out with all i was!
my story, my story.
i remember light.

TEN POEMS ON DEPRESSION

1. WHEN I'M NOT HERE
SEPTEMBER 8

life
seems dead, as bleached and gray as
smoke, the burning or
that whale we found on the beach
the gravel in my pocket

i haven't been here long but i'm not
sure i want to stay
this pressure is
real, it is not for

the sky
the empty ears
the wavering lines of love

i don't know where i am when
i'm not here

2. THE SINKING
September 9

it often comes in mid afternoon
the sinking
all the patchy places in my will
begin to come apart
i have to remind myself

this is only time
only a day, nothing else
it doesn't mean anything
the hopeless brittle afternoon

everywhere everywhere
someone is wailing in grief
all the sorrow of the world
pressure on my sternum

i cannot catch my breath

3. YOU DIDN'T KNOW WHAT TO SAY
September 10

i drove near the edges
you gathered your thoughts
you didn't know what to say
no one does
though there is so much love
i can't feel it
it doesn't seem real.

4. I HAVE WALKED ON THAT EDGE
September 11

    we aren't really equipped for this,
    for these moments of
    trying to convince one another
    to live
    we are made more for
    watching geckos
    wrestle on the ceiling
    or watching leaves dance
    where does the cup of poison
    come from? why do we wait
    and wait
    for it to withdraw
    trying to behave as though
    it is not there.
    you don't know what to say
    because how could you?
    how could i, though i have
    walked on that
    edge in the gray afternoon
    in the unforgiving glare
    of my own self-loathing.

5. TWO RESCUES
September 12

on this day
we rescued both a cicada
and
a sparrow,
two trapped beings
the cicada a creature from a laughing
God's imagination
linked exoskeleton fitted
like armor, in motion
a mask on its face like a truck grill
it waved through the window
help me
i can see the outside but
can't get there
we took it to the sky and lifted it up
the cicada flew to the top of our tallest tree
we watched it go

and the sparrow barely needed
any help at all,
after some confused moments it
found its way
to the open window
its strong bird wings took it away.

these two small things
free.

6. MAGNETS
September 13

    i prayed all day for you.

    the power went out again
    at night, just before bed
    it was hot
    so we lay on the pavement
    and looked at the sky

    on either side of me
    the kids—Solo, Isaac
    Kenya, Leafy

    (*are you scared?* Kenya
    whispered to Isaac.
    not anymore, he said. *why would*
    i be scared when i'm in between
    the two women of our
    family?)

    we pretended,
    again,
    to be magnets on the side of
    a fridge

    gazing out at the sky
    i thought of you
    when i looked at the stars behind the stars

    there is so much
    to see
    so many stars to fall into,

we could look at them forever
make a million beautiful dreams.

stay,
please stay.

7. DON'T LISTEN TO THEM
September 14

people say such terrible things
on forums and screens
threads and pages

shhh, i want to say.
talk in whispers
say holy words, the kind that
don't spike the unwary reader
or listener

no one who hasn't felt it can know
don't listen to them

they found something they could
shift away from
put a name to
decided if they can blame it on you
it won't touch them

but they are wrong
it can happen to anyone so don't listen
to those people
just turn your face to
the kindness of
evening.

8. YOU WILL LIVE AND NOT DIE
September 15

vigils need candles
so i made some

humming over the wax
as it settled

you will live and not die

no more fear
no more terror

let the healing wings close
around you
turn your face into their softness

live.

9. THOUSANDS OF WAYS
September 16

every part of me today
is life
life is the rising and falling
the painful dip in the heart
i found so much
comfort in an apple
today
in eating
i saw light everywhere
and i called to the world
to stop being afraid
to lift itself from its
inward curl
the endless cycle of fear and blame
there is no measuring here
there are thousands of ways
to live a life
you can sail it
or sit in the grass, write or
calculate rows of numbers
sing or be quiet
but you get to be
you get to exist, even after years
even if you've been trying to
achieve, to master, to win
even if you've been walking
not getting anywhere
all you need to do
is be
and in the blue of evening,
to live.

10. SEARCHING FOR CLUES
September 17

leafing through photographs
searching for clues,
there you are, smiling,
laughing
making a crazy face
you knew how to have fun,
that too, was you.
then you lost track of how
to do your hair
there were a few awkward photos
those also were you
and then the lost times
with a wild terror
somewhere behind your eyes
you forgot how to feed yourself
you looked at others and wondered
how they knew
how they woke up
and knew what it meant to be
how they dressed themselves
found friends
felt okay inside.
you didn't know,
that also, was you.
and then the slow building
a cup of tea in your hands
chopped vegetables
a radiant smile on the beach
climbing out, finding words
sun on the stones
birds in the backyard,

you at peace,
this also is you.
this is you.

NIGHT DRIVE
September 18

i drove slowly, peacefully,
i drove my motorbike at night
there was a birthday party
and i was late. i took a wrong turn
and drove for a while
along dark roads
lit by single streetlights
or village homes
it was hot
doors were open
dogs chased me
i saw people sitting on the floor
or in hammocks
or spilling onto porches
circled around bowls of rice on mats.
i smelled leaves burning
and breezes from the underside of
damp leaves or cooling
rice fields. came across some men
searching a field by torchlight,
stooping again and again
what are you catching? i asked
they showed me a bucket of crabs
i left them catching food in that field
for this village
this is food for my senses
all the light, the darkness,
the crickets and frogs in the humid night.

OPEN MIC
September 19

>Leafy and i drove through the dark night
>to listen to his dad play music—
>either of us could happily
>cozy up inside on a Saturday
>but the thought of Chinua on keys
>and Cricket on saxophone called us out
>Leafy watched intently, listening
>i watched him watching, proud
>of his very existence
>when it was time for the open mic,
>he decided to play—an old song,
>a familiar one
>i kept waiting for him to change his mind,
>but he walked up there,
>sat down, and played his song
>and we all listened to this boy play
>hands on the keys, mind in the music.
>i was proud of his very existence.

MOTHER'S PRAYER
September 20

God of sleepless nights and
mothers who have hearts of fire and fear,
keep us.
we are lost without you.
we are terrified without you.
take our early morning hearts
and soothe them. bring us bright angels,
lions around our children, pacing,
growling, protecting.
keep our babies
out of the jaws of death.
help us not to despair.
help us to say the words of comfort
to keep on when we are the only ones who know
how terrified we feel. wipe our tears.
speak kindly to us. remind us of the times
we did so well, we took care of everyone
though we could hardly rest.
we need your strong hands.
we need you to lull us to sleep with
promises of better days ahead.

MORNING AFTER A BAD NIGHT
September 21

the familiar red concrete floor
with the sheen of many years
bare feet on this ground, toes
and the earth walls.

last night was a bad one.

only a few people came at first
and then, one after the other,
this friend and that
Ro jumped up to get bowls of food
the three dogs greeted one another
and we played with the three-year-old girl

i heard Spanish being spoken,
Thai, and Swiss German. soft voices

my friend held my hand when i told
her that things have been harder than usual.
she taught my sons more nunchuck tricks
a bit of hooping. soft voices.

a long afternoon with
the light slowly changing
i made chai with mint and soy milk,
you wouldn't imagine it was delicious but
it was—we took seconds.

RAINBOW
September 22

i left to pick Solomon up from his class—
late again, but as i left, the rainbow—so close!
reminded me of life away from clocks.
the rainbow followed me around the valley
and when i found my son
he was playing with his friends
all was well.
we drove home on the motorbike and i prayed
in the golden light, the dark stormy sky
a backdrop of every leaf edged with gold.
i prayed for golden light for him,
and for every child everywhere.

GETTING READY TO LEAVE
September 23

we're pretty funny
packing for a trip. always
a few instruments, last minute
jars of almonds or chia seeds,
questions about toys, bicycles.

the car itself is not even ready,
still dawdling in the shop getting tires
and a new air filter.

then, i might start giving the instruction to
get in the car! an hour before we go,
maybe more than once.
we don't leave,
we strap things to the roof,
bring a trumpet, a clarinet, a piano
and a cast-iron skillet. kiss our pup
goodbye and herd everyone in. finally.

after a few minutes of driving
we realize someone
forgot his shoes, and go back to retrieve them.
we lose luggage off the roof and pick it up
from the road. we caravan loosely.
we can't get windows to go back up.
we get rained on and take slow shortcuts.

it is not until we arrive at our destination,
three hours later, that we find
a second shoeless person in our midst,
a kid who got in the car without thinking
about his feet, and must now walk barefoot
on city streets.

BIG CITY
September 24

Isaac in the grocery store
is a sight to behold.
we don't have big stores
in our village, so when i take him
with me in the city he walks with
eyes like plates
dancing beside the cart or
pushing it with
every bit of might he has
in his little boy arms,
careening into water bottles,
reading signs
asking for oranges,
drinking a drink from the vending machine
for the very first time!
helping and chatting and
charming people.
and it doesn't end
when we are done,
because then he has to
tell everyone at home
about the grocery store.

IN THE HOSPITAL
September 25

in the hospital,
men in hospital pajamas
sit or lie on blue
vinyl-covered benches
and smile when we come in.
we walk between them
they are like the old
kings of Gondor
fallen on hard times
the aisle between them
the river, we are on a boat
sailing toward our friend
eager to find him.

BREONNA
September 26

Breonna Taylor
should be alive

though
she was born into an unkind world
an unkind history, white supremacy
and the War on Drugs

now people pick apart
her innocence (stop it)
after bullets killed her.
bullets from where? they are unclaimed,
from who? they are innocent bullets
from nowhere?

no one
is to blame and yet
she is the only one
not still with us
in a room full of men
she she she she she she
alone fell.

angels come!
close the mouths of the lions
so they can't talk about her.
discussing the ins and outs
and who did what

she was home.
she had walked through the day
the innumerable dangers

and arrived in a safe place.
home.

they opened the door
to a safe place
and took away safety
and life
in a few short minutes

she should be alive
and she is dead
and no one is held responsible.

this is not a discussion.
this is the soul leaving
the body
a body that had not yet done
all it was meant to do,
a life.

"if a slave should die while being corrected
the master will be acquitted of punishment
or accusation
but if the slave lift his or her hand—
thirty lashes" Virginia Code 1705,
(paraphrased)

this is about the body.

we have said—
white people
this is our history
—do not look away,

if i do something to you,
i will go free.
if you do something to me,
you will be punished

and it lands
on women, Black women,
working with their hands
in the same way every other person
washes dishes, tidies the living room,
pays the bills,
gets by,

a cold wall of white men at the door

murder with
bullets from protected guns that
won't be taken
hands that won't be disarmed
it will happen again and
they will not help you.

everywhere chattering with all they know—
they try to rearrange these
facts, to explain that they know
they know better
but this is poison
it is poisoning us,
stealing our humanity and

her body.
her body was hands and arms and
soft skin, soft organs, a rib cage
the heart, keeping it all together.
eyes that saw the world and dreamed
a body that was a little girl
and then a woman for such
a short time.

the body is itself.
the body belongs to God and itself.
no one else.
the body is not for someone else's profit

not for someone else's contempt
or judgment — God made Breonna's body
housed it with breath and love
made it with melanin
made it with glory

angels come!
the body is home
the house is home
and where can Black women be safe?

if she closed the door, put up her feet?
was she safe?

if you close your door, put up your feet?
are you safe?

what is this myth of the safe place?
of private property and the right to protect

angels come now!
with fire
i call you, make them stop
dissecting moments and angles and
their exhausting opinions,
every word they utter
like a whitewashed tomb
nothing inside but decay
their contempt for the body,
for the Black body, for women
for Black women, the home of the body
the delicate rib cage, like a house
for a jewel,
their belief that they know better than God.

VIGIL
September 27

the hospital has hallways,
nurses, friends. trees outside the
window, flowers, bad food.
old men peering into the windows.
it's part of us, now
we will never forget this vigil—
the sheen
of floors, light on the walls,
boxes of unwanted soy milk. music,
games, Minecraft obstacle courses with
visitors, each day long and speckled
with light and sadness
a step toward healing
a long walk
oh, such a long walk.

LUCKY
September 28

*there's nothing wrong or right
in conversation,* i say, just before they
walk into the building. *you can say whatever
you want.*
they don't believe me. why should they—
the whole world tells them they
need to find the phrase that will ensure
they are neither too different nor too much
the same, neither stupid nor too smart,
i wish i could unravel it all, make them
see and feel their golden souls
that this world is lucky to have them
lucky even to catch sight of their spinning
dance.

TO REALLY SEE
SEPTEMBER 29

Gax is over eighty and invites my son for
a bike ride. *just fifteen kilometers,* he says,
and then an amazing breakfast.
then fifteen kilometers back.
we are eating dinner at the table.
Kai lives with this man and
his wife, my friend.
she married him, a widower, nearly forty years ago—
she was eighteen years younger
and they lived in an older Thailand
with food still wrapped only in banana leaves
their stories are well worn and bright
she's so smart, he says when she leaves the
table. *she never stops learning, she's always*
gathering new things, new information
and ideas. she brings me with her. even if i
don't want to go. and then he laughs.
i don't know if my son sees
the depth in this love,
the offering of companionship
of intellect, care, and conversation
but i hope he gathers it up and holds it
that he keeps this new information,
that he can pull it out later
well worn and shiny,
and really see.

FOR LEAF
September 30

i want you to find rest
and light in this world. i wish
for sunsets, birds on the wing
long walks on the beach. i want you to
feel God-breath
your angel's wings
around you. i wish you
quiet limbs, deep sleep, an old day
with large trees and golden light
playing with shadow. goodness.
peace. watching your son surf.
taking all the drawings your daughter
will bring to you, filling your lap,
all the flowers. i wish for a boat to carry
you dreaming, i wish for your sisters
to surround you. i want your song
to soar from your throat, for all your
birds to sing along with you, for
your dreams to be sweet and good and
true. i want you to grow old with
these days as only faint memories
of times that were hard, so hard,
with bars on the windows and
that one old man who wouldn't stop
interfering, rating each day out
of ten, the coldness of the floor,
the fragility
and the loss of our dreams
no no, just faint memories
that show how precious all these
good things are. cinnamon days,
friends who love you, a light heart in

the morning, your husband's hands,
temple bells,
bare feet, i wish you whales, thousands
of them, breaching and crashing
into the water, diamond drops
in the air.

OCTOBER 2020

ON YOUR BIRTHDAY
October 1

in the evening light,
on your birthday,
i looked at your face
and thought, *i have you.*
only you.
marriage is good,
i said, and you said, *yes.*
i'm not sure if you caught
that i meant that we at least
will be together, always.
i cannot be sure of much else
in this world. maybe
you understood
or, maybe there was a deeper
meaning in you, when you said
yes, maybe
you were saying yes to the light
or the water, the sky, or us, all of our
years together
or maybe you remembered the day
we met or the lake where we rowed.
maybe it was just the light there
on your face on your birthday
there with our children
and us, after these years
a good day,
the day you were born.

A THOUSAND MOMENTS
October 2

today i went through old photos,
today i looked at my face in a thousand
moments, children spilling out of my arms,
sitting and holding them always,
heavy

my arms don't want to let go

i kissed my son's face in the middle of the street,
had to reach way up to do it
gave him herbal concoctions—
i could see that he was humoring me

do i have any other shape
than the curving, protective shape?
do i even know how to walk with
my heart out?

the miles and barriers between here and there
i don't know, this has been a hard year

my legs go numb because of two people
sitting in the scoop of lap that is mine
i am more comfy than the concrete floor,
callouses on my ankles, my aching arms

they don't want to let go.

SAY THE REAL WORDS
October 3

tell me the truth,
please,
not only sometimes. you may
think the story is yours to tell
how you want it, that the earth is
yours to mold
but no, it was molded long ago
the days will be as they
are
and you cannot keep telling
us false stories. i throw down the phone

i want truth!
i, the storyteller, i try to tell
true stories, though they are sometimes
make-believe, there is no trick, no gotcha
no *you thought you knew what you knew*
but now the floor is falling

i know what i want, i want truth
so rare and whole, so perfect, like
cold water on a hot day,

a stream of the real, floating by
a conveyor belt of solid and actual things.

you must stop using your voice for lies
we are not the story you are writing
with your half-hidden malice

this table before me is truth.
my hands, my existence

that man at another table reaching
for his coffee
the dog in the parking lot

my longing for truth,
my longing not to be lied to, grows
into a tree
mighty within me

small globes of real things grow from
its branches. love. sorrow. disappointment. joy.
i hold it reverently, gently, my longing
bending my body. tell us the truth! stop
lying! stop sowing our beds with distrust

but even if you cannot say truth things

we will know
we will know what is real and God will hold
our real stories, gently, like small, precious spheres.

THE PAINT ON THE WALLS
October 4

the green of this ward can
hardly be named. mint? i guess?
lime sherbet? yesterday they set up
table tennis in the main corridor
and when i left, a man with his
shirt off demanded that i play.
i declined politely, then
more assertively when it seemed
i might not get by.
he was a wild one. the other men in
the ward usually just nodded in greeting.
one young guy with tattoos
complimented my hair.
and then there were
the two angels at the beginning
who visited with reassurance
and snacks to share.
i wonder where the women's ward is
and what color is the paint
on their walls.

MOTORBIKE IN THE CITY
October 5

    in this great big city
    in the north of Thailand
    people still forage for greens
    in ditches on the sides
    of highways
    there are raintrees
    spreading their branches
    over billboards and buildings
    scraps of old posters
    bright new signs

    in between multi-storied
    blocks of shops and homes
    crossed by layers of wire
    you can see hidden stupas
    or temple spires

    i sit at traffic lights on the
    motorbike for what
    feels like hours, the sun
    scorching my skin—
    every other person on a bike
    nearby is wearing a jacket
    for this reason,
    but i cannot bear it
    my freckles widen, i tap my feet
    beside me a man and his wife
    pull up in a motorbike with a sidecar
    brimming with garden tools
    i smile at them and they smile
    back, the light turns green and with a

roar of many engines we drive.
i am feeling at home now.

FEVER!
October 6

      i drove in the rain
      on the motorbike
      i knew i shouldn't do it
      sat soaked in the hospital room
      for a few hours
      air conditioning shivers
      made puddles on the floor
      from my sodden clothes

      people here in Thailand
      used to say to me
      fever, fever!
      when Isaac was a baby
      if i let his head get wet in the rain

      they were right
      you can't say i didn't know better
      and so i got sick
      and then i tried to be healthy
      because it wasn't a good time
      to be sick

      now i am
      ready for sleep
      and
      no more driving in the rain.

WHAT I AM WRITING ALL THE TIME
October 7

the rain pounded the street outside
but i was inside with my coffee
and my thoughts.
the barista wore his hair long
and started to recognize me after
a few days. art on foam, the
quiet clicking of keys. the men
murmuring to one another behind
the counter, undulating Thai language.
i recognized words here and there
but put my headphones on
this has always been the most blissful
thing. i was the only foreigner,
everyone buried in their work, and
words came, one after another,
they left my mind—my middle mind, the
one that barely knows, that always
surprises me—the words moved house
lugged their suitcases
onto the screen
into the world.
i love you and love you.
it's actually what i am writing,
all the time.

DISTRACTING OURSELVES
October 8

she tells me so many things.
unicorns don't usually have wings
but special ones do. some have gold horns
this one lives in a special place.
we will make a whole origami group of friends
they will love each other.
i am getting a new puppy.

i have no favorite color.

i told her about my friend
who always says that her favorite color
is polka-dot

scientists say, she tells me very seriously
that polka-dots make you happy

the rabbit who used to be named earless
has ears now and is named fearless
fearless is good friends with the other rabbit—
the one called
mynah. i remember mynah rabbit from
long ago, when we went hiking,
mynah rabbit used to poke her ears
out of her father's backpack
the ears flopped around
i still have a photo somewhere

i took pictures
we always knew she was magical
we always knew she was clever

i was in the kitchen when i heard that her
mother—my friend— was expecting her.
my kids came running
when i shrieked for joy
we always knew she would one day
boss us around, we knew we would do
whatever she ordered us to do

i think of this as i hide under a table
in the corner
with the spiders. she is searching for me
and we are distracting ourselves from
the sadness of moving away.

THE HONEST STARS
October 9

there wasn't much that could be done
to make this more difficult
pandemic, harrowing urgent move
packed in a week. we have mustered
every single thing. Ro organized

an army of supportive owls
and other night birds
they fluttered close and packed the things
nestled us close
made us breakfast in the morning

there was so much loss
we couldn't even think about it
the concept of never. we closed our ears
and played music instead. cuddled with
clouds and llamas, danced through open
windows into trees that always caught
us when we fell

we cried at various moments in the day
wrapped in grief like magician's capes
the honest stars in their skies
old songs and all the losses
adding up and taking away
—math games.

GOODBYE GATHERING
October 10

the children danced
and shrieked. we talked,
drank tea or wine coolers
ate food. the music was also
our food. Chinua sang and sang.
sometimes Leaf joined him,
for a while there were 80's
singalongs. we sat in the garden.
the children looked for us but
we pretended we weren't there
for a little while. the singing went on
we tossed flowers
everyone hugged. Kenya
sat
and dreamed

BRAVE AND HEARTBROKEN
October 11

well, no.
this was not the way
i imagined it.
two dogs
thirteen kids and
many red-eyed adults
at the airport
in a pandemic. none of us
could have foreseen this
part of the journey
we drove straight from the
hospital to the airport
the car was full of love.
Isaac was excited about
junk food. there were talks
and hugs but
it was too sad.
we cried too much
and for too long. we prayed
too, but we cried. they
looked so brave and heartbroken
as they were walking away.

ALL MOSTLY OKAY
October 12

after a long day
Leafy walked through the glass door
he walked through it
not over it or around it
he did not slide the door
he walked through it and
we all heard the crash and
came running
we all heard the glass splintering
hitting the floor, and came
running
and there he was, surprised and woozy
it could have been so much worse
he had a few cuts because
panes of glass are not meant
to be walked through
but other than our nerves
which were shattered
and the door
which was shattered
we were all mostly okay.

HAIR STORIES
October 13

let me try to tell this
story because i know you will ask.

or maybe you will be too polite
to ask. or maybe you don't care. i will
tell the story anyway. that is part of it.

hair is just hair. and also not.
when i was young people in school
made fun of my hair for being fluffy
curly. big. curly hair was not the thing.
side ponytails, sleek and smooth
were the thing.

this doesn't matter.

i cut it and grew it and cut it and grew it.
it became a barometer, a way to tell
what changes were happening. when i
left the beach and the mountains, when i
moved into the Victorian and the rest of my
life, i cut it off in the bathroom. the man
who would become my husband watched me
do it. i was daring him to still like me. i was
grieving the life i had left behind.

we traveled continents and slept on ships
i wore scarves and used showers that were
just pipes in the walls. i got lice
and combed them out. i evaded
glances and hands as well as i could.
he proposed on an island under the moon.

my hair was curly there, happy in the humidity
of that tropical place.

i wore it pinned up at our wedding, curls
around my face. his hair was short
we had cut his dreadlocks off in the jungle. lice—
we threw the hair into the woods.
we got married, him with short hair,
me with my curls. we drove
away as happy as we have ever been

we went to many weddings
and soon i found that i was pregnant. my hair
got curlier. we moved to a little house by a marsh,
he practiced kung fu in the morning with our
housemates. we lived and worked with
need, there was always need, always people at the
door, always so much joy. my belly grew
and i wanted to escape. i decided to lock my hair
to be bound to my people, to the need, to the
discomfort.

and they grew alongside one another,
my dreadlocks and my baby
and i grew up too. at the coin laundry
with the diapers, in the co-op babywearing,
looking in windows wistfully at things
from another life
my hair short, like a nest of disgruntled birds

two more children, trips up the stairs in a back
alley, eating cereal while standing,
trips across the country, tents in the woods
my dreadlocks grew longer
and i loved it more. a fourth pregnancy,
a flight overseas, a birth in a rainy wilderness
four children and it was long and lovely. we lived
in another world. we have never left.

i shaved an undercut in India, at a tiny little
barbershop on the side of the road
babywearing again,
in the mountains this time.
Chinua was in Turkey and i
needed to do something about the heat.
people warned me that it was
the first step to cutting them all off and
they were right but it took longer than they thought—
ten more years

during which we traveled and Kenya's locks also grew
and we were
beautiful with the same kind of hair
we saw the world together and i helped her evade
glances and hands—
she was so beautiful. that has been us. a tight family

all these growing up years, the fifth child, a surprise
after a trip to Laos in the hot season
i have adjusted myself
to motherhood and those around me
again and again, settled into changes, seen people
come and go, cried far too many times. i have been
known like this. i have been constant. blond locks.
maybe a hat. a troupe of kids who grew taller

i long for it all. it doesn't feel fair that it
is going by now, that i have lost my younger self
and i know i cannot keep any of this—
youthful husband or self, lack of pain in our bodies
place in the world.
we have been alone in this pandemic
and i have felt my solitude within the shelter
of my family, of womanhood

so finally, i cut my dreadlocks off
after eighteen years, and i am changed

i look like i did when i first went to India
with the addition of twenty years to
my face that stares back at me from the mirror
blond ringlets, remembering the laughter of middle school,
the cries of *whoa, afro!* when all i wanted was
to fit in. how poor that girl's view of the world was,
for fitting in to be the dream

that dream was short, thankfully, it didn't
take much more than a year or so before i knew
it was no good, no amount of gel
could cure a wild heart, i have come this far
hair is just hair, but something lately
tells me that all of life is about change and letting go
and by cutting my hair i have found a way to say:
i am ready for it.

I HOPE YOU REMEMBER THE DREAM
October 14

waking at the end of a long absence
the heart lurches toward something
normal, where are we now?
home, where is home? we're going
home on a bus today. we're driving the
curves today. we're hugging our family
today.

we're in the air
floating until we touch down
somewhere different
the bus wheels spin, so much has
changed from what it was
everyone is taller, maybe even
sadder

do you remember the dream?
i hope you remember the dream.
we left the city and found our valley
just as small and perfect
as it has ever been.

THE MELODY IN MY HEAD
October 15

i awoke at home and did these small things:
brushed teeth, walked outside and looked
at the view. sat at my desk with a cup of coffee—
a morning indulgence—said, i love you i love you
i love you i love you. patted the dogs, watched the
chickens—who have grown up here—arguing with the
mynahs over the compost heap

(right now there are five in there,
all grown now, and colorful. fatter than the other
neighborhood chickens. i tell myself that they are this
lovely because of the superior quality of our compost heap
grubs.)

i wrote a poem and wish i could have written a song
one day i will have the language for song,
these comforting things deserve a melody—
in my head it lifts and falls, lifts and falls.

YOU ARE NOT FINISHED
OCTOBER 16

you are not finished
in the long story of your life.
you are curled like a leaf
under the light of
God's regard,
gentle eyes,
tender gaze.

you are on a hillside in the late afternoon
all the grasses bending toward you
all the Spirit's songs reaching for you.

look up

that sky is yours
look at the blue of it
you are loved and this great expanse
offers itself to you
your words can fill it
your singing can exult there.
even after a whole notebook
of tired days, the scattered papers of years—
you are delightful and cared for and new.

will you soften into the hillside?
will you let your bones rest?
lay your heart down
and forget your attempts to wring
what you wanted out of these days
forget the ways you faltered
and flailed.

look at you now,
so beautiful among the flowers.

TWENTY-TWO POEMS ON HOME

1. BEDSHEET
October 17

in India, when i was nineteen years old,
i bought a bedsheet
in the desert.
i had only seen them
—these gorgeous, colorful, extravagant cloths—
on walls.
but they were bedsheets, i was told.
we put them on our beds, said the man at the stall.
his mustache was glorious.

it was hot that day,
the scent of incense and burning dung
filling the air,
the sun gripping my skull like a vice.
i was unsure of everything.
my heart was blooming like a rose.

i was drawn to the red sheet
with the yellow dots
i smoothed my hands over it
bought it

by the lake the women called to me
wanting to henna my hands,
men tried to sell us flowers
a donkey called out in the street.
i felt longing like i had never
known before.

after that, i spread that sheet
on every bed in every guest house

or hostel. and it, with my backpack
and my books,
became my home.

2. BEFORE
October 18

before, i remember these homes:

the house on the hill where i painted my room
as a teenager—
the ultimate freedom, to make giant green ferns
on my walls. i had a window seat, where i sat
looking at other homes, lights in their windows,
dreaming. i loved it there.

the house in the cornfield,
the tent trailer in many provinces and states
while we traveled, so free
the tent in the rain
my grandparents' house

and before that
the house on the street where i ran
for the bus. the trees around the houses
the park with the huge sprinklers

coffee in the kitchen
Anne of Green Gables
my grandparents' fabric store
my mom's cooking
music on the record player
movies with nachos, phones with cords
playing dress-up, the lawn in front of the
house in Mission, icy creeks
touques and mittens.

my sister and brothers and
working in the car with my dad at night.

Mom laughing. dark afternoons. snow.
the lake in Kelowna, the church floor in
San Diego. the big white van.
my mind, which was growing to
fit the whole world
and so many kinds of homes.

3. AFTER
OCTOBER 19

    after the Indian bedsheet
    there was the red kettle.
    actually no,
    after the Indian bedsheet,
    there was you.
    the place between your face and
    your shoulder, where
    my head finds its home.

4. OUR CABIN
October 20

okay, and then,
home.
our cabin. our new home together
all the nights we spent holding onto
one another.
the egrets in trees beyond the bridge
the marsh and the Indian restaurant.
our babies. a graffitied alleyway
a very full house, full of conversation
heartbreak, discussion, meals.
a little lost.
a river
that called my soul out of its body
every day. trees. trees and wildflowers.
singing around the fire. growing up
slowly.
and then the warm wood floors and that
red kettle. the red kettle that i called home.
it was mine. i chose it. i didn't pull it from
a pile on the curb, or have it
handed down to me. i saw it
loved it
bought it. i used it every day
and it was home to me.
for tea in the morning, for coffee
for the pregnancy tea that tasted
like hay.

5. THE RED KETTLE
October 21

the red kettle. during the years
of the red kettle, i began to know
myself, look— the beams of my home
were so shaky, permeable.
there were wide gaps
the skeleton could have shook me
to pieces i was not at home
inside i was not able to sleep
if another person knocked on
these hollow walls, demanding
to be let in, i always let them in.

God's voice was often lost in the
howling winds i allowed within me.
i was ragged and tear-stained
though also sometimes joyful, it was
not that there was no joy,
the beauty was immense.
but the ripples of fear threatened
to consume me.

6. THE STORY
October 22

it was then that i began to tell
the home story. every
time i sat in front of the fire with
yarn and needles in my hands,
and then told about it,
was like another board or
touch of paint.

to be at home in myself
was still a very long way off
but i can see now
this was the beginning.

dance was there in this time
and this was home too.

some voices at this time said
you are not at home.
you don't know what you think you know.

i have learned to ignore these voices
but then
they were gales that shook the house
they shook me to my core.

that house—the real one—
fell after we left it.
there was no looking back.

DOVES
October 23

we took everything
in bags and boxes
to a new country.

i watched doves dive, boneless
and felt as though i was falling, too.
home was nebulous
fragile,
lost.

8. JAYA
October 24

first the jungle in India.

i had not yet learned how
not to
shake myself apart, and i rattled
to my teeth.

my body was still a home
to my fourth child. he must have
felt the rafters creak. i hoped he
was dreaming through it.

Jaya then,
the unlikely home i didn't expect.
her voice in the kitchen,
calm hands in the market.
sitting on the porch together
telling me her stories
showing me
how to gather and prepare
how to find a home in food
in India
in the daily things
in turmeric facial masks, painting
Kenya's nails, making the roti
the graceful art of sweeping
with one hand behind your back.

i looked for home and could not
find it. she found it for me.
told me about the monitor lizards
that the village people would eat

the monkeys clattered on the tiles.
she ate whole chilies.

in the morning there was
Jaya, with her long black hair
and her housedresses.

i rested beside her until i could take
a breath.

9. YOU BUILD AGAIN
October 25

what happens is you build again.
comforts grow
you find the thing that feels like now
like home—
putting your face in the
cardamom jar
and inhaling.
daily chai.
a favorite brand of biscuit.

you don't know when the change happens

but on the other side, you know
how to feed yourself—
something you have never really
known—you know the translucent change
of onions breaking down in a pan
you can roll roti
you are less shaky.
the structure of your
days takes shape, the breath
of each hour becomes like an old song
one you have heard
in a language you understand,
you know which tomatoes will be
the best, which aubergines are
ripe,
you hear the horn of the bread man
and run out to greet him.

10. THE BIRTH
October 26

then, the birth
and home is centered anew on this
little family
in the sand,
with the beach dogs who trail you
always hopeful always
waiting—the children too,
your own and the others,
their hair grows
and their limbs
the little one starts to walk
Leafy hugs the coconut trees
you can barely stand the heat
but in the water you hug
your little ones and kiss them
over and over again.

the rooftop.
light slanting across the red floor
the light tones of voices speaking German,
the afternoon coffee and chocolate
—you are home, this has become your home.

the trains, the red head wraps of the porters as
they run ahead of you, feet flashing
your children trying to keep up
you follow, carrying the baby
eyes on
the porters with their heads so high
they bob with each step
to handle the weight of the bags on
their heads.

they lead you straight to your berth
where you make nests for
your little ones to curl up in
you feed the baby bits of curried potato
his white top stained yellow
you are home
this has become your home.

11. THE MOUNTAINS
October 27

i met the mountains in the afterward
they sang to me
the sweetest songs of forests
and straight limbed trees
i wept for the goat bells, held the
hands of the woman who came each day
to drink my chai, sweep my floors
and play with the baby.
the Irish man downstairs
scolded my children when they
quarreled. my son and daughter climbed the
rocks like goats. we ran straight down
mountains, then came back after
burdened with our groceries,
wrapped in paper sacks.
we ate chocolate cake
there was only one kind. the trees
nodded over our heads. the fog
came close.

12. THE BANYAN
October 28

later, much later,
we put in the garden.
the garden designer was a
small man with large glasses
and big dreams. his passion was
the grass
it will be like a carpet, he declared
he enunciated each word: like. a. carpet.

i still think those words when
i look at grass, and wonder, what was this man's
experience with carpets?

while they prepared the expanse
in front of that pink house
each day was dustier than the one before

the workers—a collection of women and
men from a neighboring state, stopped working
if the garden designer left for the day
the women choosing instead to sit in the dust
and braid Kenya's hair.

i watched through the window
unwilling to interrupt.
Kenya sorted shells and laid them in
patterns, and two or more women
smoothed back her dreadlocks,
weaving them together into thick plaits.

i made them tea, or sometimes Jaya did it.

by then i had learned the lesson of the banyan—
a big tree in every village:
to stop and rest in the shade
to sit when you can sit
that there is nothing wrong with simply
watching, doing nothing else at all.

SO MANY LOVES
October 29

Miriam was there. Johanna, too, these
two women who loved us and told us stories
of their days. we all adored Solomon when
he was a baby. we jumped around in the waves.

there were so many loves. Cate and her paints,
the standing babies, Maria and Rosario next door,
the goats in the grove, the sea eagles
who caught snakes and fed them to their babies
in the nest.

we lived in Nepal, also,
at the skirts of the highest mountains
in the world. i cooked in so many cities
shopped in so many markets
looking for the most beautiful potatoes
searching for fresh spinach.
passing money with two hands
my left fingers touching my right wrist.

i woke up and wrote, no matter
how tired, no matter how busy my mind.

the water lapping at the shore,
the kids in the park, the stones on the walkways
corn growing beside the path. these were all stories
in them we were home. we found each other there,
we found God there, we became a home

the stories held us when we had to leave.

14. ROOTS
October 30

we left the pink house near the coconut grove.
left the country of India.

the trains in Thailand were so cold they
felt like a fridge. we shivered under towel
covers, but the people were so kind, offering snacks,
carrying the babies
so we could rest.

i gave birth to Isaac in a hospital in Chiang Mai.
my mom read books on my porch and held him
when i needed a break.
i was always surrounded by flowers. there
has been a permanent longing for somewhere else
lodged in my heart for so many years, and certainly

during the months of this pandemic
so i turn in circles looking at the brown earth
home. i say. home. looking for the roots of
tiny animal-like plants. home.
looking at the faces of my growing children
home. the husband i met when i was only
eighteen years old. home.

the garden, home now for so many years
these light conversations, the ones that go deeper
in widening circles, we are all turning.
i could run forever.
i could run looking, yelling
calling, laughing. home.

i see the look in the face of my daughter
and know we have given her, also
this old story of loving and longing.

15. THE WAY IT SHOWS UP
October 31

    home will hit you like love.
    like long, tearful talks
    or perfect evening songs.
    like kids piled onto one another
    or monitor lizards crawling up
    riverbanks. trees losing their hardened
    leaves, it will hit like dreams
    that don't quite go the way you
    thought they would. or like a gift
    from a friend. like a hug.
    like a surprise.
    in a way, home never fully arrives
    but it shows up again and again.

NOVEMBER 2020

16. THE MOON
NOVEMBER 1

    the night of the full moon
    and the lanterns that fly
    over the mountains,
    i sat on the riverbank
    letting out my sorrow.
    crying loudly enough
    that the moon could hear me
    her reflection was just the tiniest
    glimmer on the water
    her light edging toward me
    through the trees.

    home hits you like this, too.

17. THE SHIFT
November 2

when i came to this country
people loved the king enough to
cross-stitch his image onto a piece
of cloth—four feet by eight.

when he died, we wore black for a year.

now, well, no one cross-stitches
portraits of the new king. people hold three
fingers up when he drives by
and crowds stand against the police
in the streets, holding umbrellas against
chemical-infused rain. it is not
the same anymore

home shifts under your feet
you move and you don't stop moving.

18. HAPPINESS
November 3

a moment i go back to,
just because i soaked it in:

sitting at the papaya salad shop
on the side of the road. this was
the first one, with the older couple.
their daughter was a nurse at the hospital.

it was April, the hottest month
and my skin felt dry and windblown
like August in California.

the light made shadows through
the bamboo fence. dust rose when the
puppies rolled on the ground. there were
flowers growing over the roof.

i sat in front of the weak-willed fan
and watched
the auntie make my food.

someone
came and gave the dogs bits of meat
they wriggled all over with happiness.

19. THE VOTES
NOVEMBER 4

(today we held our breath.
we are in the future here, many time
zones ahead. i found Chinua somewhere around
midday *"doesn't look good,"* he said

"but Detroit," we breathed, *"Detroit might do it"*

we went back to watching
and refreshing)

20. DETROIT
NOVEMBER 5

what can i tell you about Detroit?
it was Chinua's home.
i was twenty-one years old the first
time i went there. newlywed. Chinua
and i held hands on the plane, guarding our
possessions- it was only a month after 9-11
and they were destroying items left on the ground
even the lost ones

i can only imagine what our family must have
been thinking. Chinua's father hugged me
straight away at the airport. our little sisters were still
just kids. we played video games in the living room
and ate Roxanne's cobbler. we went to Aunt Loretta's
house and played *bop it*. everywhere, Black art.
everywhere, Black family. i was in love with Chinua
and in love with everything.

Ethagbhe and Chinua showed me around town.
i saw the burned houses
and traced the soot patterns with
my eyes. we stayed with Aunt Brenda
and I listened to her stories. there were so many
aunts, uncles, and cousins. i looked at old
photographs at Aunt Lavon's house,
knowing nothing. i was a kid
and they didn't know me either, but they told me about
their city and their love for it. Chinua played drums
with his father in Greektown.

we've gone back many times. the family has moved around,

lived in different places. white people came in and bought the big houses in the middle of the city. my sister told me about how that hurt. how it hurts still.

21. WHAT IT HAS GROWN INTO
November 6

here is the hard part. not the making
but the keeping of home
don't topple the structure, don't dig away at the
foundation. just rest here, lovely. make a garden
water your plants. you don't need to shift it all
brick by brick, carrying it with you, heaving the
whole set of windows and the table from the
dining room.

every day, wake up.
turn in circles. greet each flower
hug your children
smile at your husband from across the room
be at home here and let it be what it is, what it
has grown into.

22. THE SHELTER
November 7

you have been my home
from before my eyes could see
from everlasting to everlasting
you
love me. wait for the dance
wait for the dawning, for the day to break
in my eyes. one day i will truly feel it all
that you have breathed in me
sheltered me, heard me again and again
waited for me in the secret.
you have been my home

today
you are my home, i walk on the earth
encased in your light, protected by
your hands on all sides. no one can
see me but you, no one can define me
but you. i wait in the shell of home
i wait for your leading. *let's go over there*
you say. *don't worry*, you whisper
i am with you.

ASSUMPTIONS
November 8

a long reptile
lurked in the tree.
blue-headed lizard
listening.
blinking slowly. breath held.
will he make it through the day?
i don't often have to wonder this
for myself
most days i assume it
i'll get to sunset without harm
my children clustered around me,
food in my belly, my bed will be
dry and on the ground and not
floating or torn away.

i hold thankfulness in my cupped hands
like water.

THE PRAYER ON THE STREET
November 9

in the morning i went to buy soap
before school was meant to start
watch a documentary, i told the boys, *i'll be right back.*
i went to the ATM first and a
a man turned his bike around to stand nearby
while i fed the numbers to the machine.
i didn't want to look at him
but he stayed and stayed, and finally i looked up.
hello! he said. *do you remember me?*
i did, though he looked different, his hair longer, wilder
a French man i met years ago
he wanted to tell me today that the world is changing now
things are happening
i won't be able to use the ATM for much longer
many words were lost in the
wilderness of his accent and eyes, the lines in his face.
i listened, and nodded. i remembered
this man. his story

his Lisu wife had a massage shop
i went there a few times long ago, when my pain
was bad. she had her own style of massage
she would attack the knots in my muscles
from far off, as though she leapt toward them
—a kind of sport. sometimes it seemed she wanted to
shake the skin off my back
today this man, her husband with the wild eyes
wanted to pray, now, right now, in the street
so we gripped hands, facing each other.

we were beside the mosque
it is a small town

everyone knows i am married to another man
but the French man needed to pray
and it is one thing i can do
i cannot calm his mind or help his
thoughts but i can pray
so we did and i asked for calm and safety and healing
he prayed for awareness.
i prayed for truth and light.

LONG-LEGGED AND HOPEFUL
November 10

sometime
after the sun came up, i heard music
outside my workroom and looked across
the lawn. my son was there. my fourth
child, Solomon of the brave eyes.
he sat on the grass with his trumpet
wearing a jacket and gloves
(the weather has turned chilly)
playing for the birds and the rice fields
i hope they love him
i hope they know what it means for him
to play for them. i hope they grow
well, hearing his music, so long-legged
and hopeful.

ON THE FLATS
November 11

down by the river,
if you walk all the way down the hill
you find the flats of the valley
workers are planting
garlic now
our valley is known for it
for our garlic and our beauty
intertwined.
the sunsets at this time of year fill the soul.
i found something like a tiny monastery
an abandoned house
and a farmer's shelter
the garlic
grew in long rows
a truck full of workers
called out as they passed me
on the dusty road
heading home in the dusk.

IT DOES NOT NEED ME
November 12

the beauty of the world is too much and
there is honestly nothing i can do with these
trees, those mountains, this light
that calls my heart so convincingly.
i cannot earn its beauty, i cannot keep it close
i can't hold the sky, no matter how it calls.
i want it i want to hug it or hold it like i
hold my daughter, i want to tell it i will do
anything for it, for the light that comes through the
trees, i will put myself in the oldest clothes
i will go without food,
i will dig if the ground needs

but no.
it is here with or without me
it does not need me to hold it up
it has not required my service
though i reach for it, though
every day it makes me long to be
better

i am limited.
i stretch out a sheet on the grass
sit down, let it soak in and pass by all at once
let it be separate, let it move
away
let it be
let it go.

THE LOST STORIES
November 13

i want to read the stories of all of the thinkers
the women who sat with their
babies at their breasts, deep in wonder
over the mysteries of heaven
the field women stooping to consider
what was in each seed. i want to know
how the old men thought
as they walked with the water buffalo
or cattle, searching the hills as the goats
jumped boulders. i want to know what the
ache in their shoulders told them about
God, how they saw the Almighty in the
silhouettes of trees. i want to read what the
children wrote in the sand, see what they
created with light and waves and shrieks
of joy. and yes, the women
the old women in the water, in the air,
and on the ground.
what do you have to show us?
where are your writings, your theses,
what did you think of the plague, the
great heartbreaking joy of wars ending
what did you think of art and injustice?
why do we only have a few of your mighty
voices, where are the stories from those
who were in the middle of it all?

FIERCE
November 14

a woman i know said my photo
should be titled *fierce*.
i see it too, the look on my face
at this time in my life
i want you to know i will
fight for my family, my friends.
gentle and fierce, i will bring them
inside the depth of this circle around me
inside the circle of flames.
the dogs are in here too
and countries i love, my adopted people
spiders and the earth. please hear
that this is what i am fierce about:
the people i love and their futures
and all their claims to the ear of God.

FLYING IN A CIRCLE
NOVEMBER 15

this year has been unreal
the pandemic stretches on, and i am
in a strange circle of untouched ground
with those who are dear to me.

the people in this country wear
masks without complaint and
nod with extra emphasis to show
goodwill, open hearts, ready to listen
closely or find ways to be close to
one another without touching.

from across the world i read the heartbreak
in families who are apart. it happens within
my own family. everyone tells everyone else
to be careful. be well. take care.

some people don't believe in the sickness

it feels as though we fly in a circle
without ever touching the ground.

we wash our hands and now they
have new machines that take your temperature
from your hand. more comfortable than a man
aiming a thermometer at your head
though that was only slightly
annoying

loneliness.

we know we are here. we don't know
what to tell the kids about what to expect

we hug each other tight. i feel for my parents
for my sister.
i can't fix anything at all.

LIFE WORK
November 16

my life work is to make thousands
of tangible kindnesses. to tell the story
of the longing of God for
his people, reattachment of limbs
to body, one working beautiful
masterpiece in all it should be,
i hear the longing and respond
to the call of God, the great cry of
love. be kind to the lost ones,
be kind to those who can't find
home in the storm. they are
buffeted within and without by
the lie of God's detachment or a
cold imperialistic smugness.

to make the truth tangible
i cut onions and garlic, cook them
while singing, dance a little
as i add the tomatoes. we dig in the
ground, sit and listen to people
wait for words to come from
mouths that speak other languages
than ours, that speak languages
of longing. eat together
eat now, come in, we love you
let's remember how loved we are.

people are so lonely, they need
a family—these are the smallest
attempts
and fumbles
to open something so beautiful

it would blind us if we saw it fully
—God's great
heart-rending call
for us to come
close, come into the circle
draw very near
and remember who we are.

THE WAY WE ARE FED
November 17

the rice is ready for harvest
and falling heavy on the stalks.
everywhere around the valley
people bend to cut it
and the sky behind them blazes
with the closing of another circle
the season of rice at its end.
yes this is the way food comes
to us, this is the way we are fed
the sway of people in the fields
their bright hats and shirts
the blue of the sky, the heaps of
gold in the fields.

FIRSTBORN
November 18

Kai is biding his time
and i am not ready.

it's an old story, and maybe it is
boring, but i am the heroine
in my story and in it

i watch my loves
drift away from me.

this tall
son of mine, the one who
made me a mother. why didn't
anyone tell me—oh, but maybe
they did and i couldn't listen

(people on the street in San Francisco
tried. i smiled and thought they
probably didn't understand that for me
time moved slowly, so slowly)

*i read about how we grow up
with our parents,*
my tall son told me one day at a café.
*it made me think of how young you
were when i was born.*

we did grow up together,
he and i.
i was often scolded, in
those early days.

grandmothers could tell
i was unsteady, that i didn't know
about socks or hats, that i had no
experience with
babies and sleeping
that Chinua and i didn't have
a cent to our name.
Kai and i grew up together

—i held him curled against me
like a bug. he kicked
and laughed. he loved music and
dancing. his eyes were large and
full of light.
he pointed at everything. he
saw everything. at the playground
he sifted sand
through his fingers
for hours. played with the water
in the bathroom sink—

turning and moving and we
turned and moved a few dozen
degrees and
he is biding his time before
he goes

maybe i will wait a few months,
to let the pandemic settle down,
he says—and there is a leap in my
chest—*but this is not my place.*

(he means this country and
the leap folds in on itself and
lands tucked very quietly in a space that
holds it softly, mutely)

yeah, i say, casually, so casually.
i can imagine you would be eager
to go.

VERSIONS OF ORION
November 19

the nights are growing cold now,
and brilliant with stars.
we are looking at the constellations
again
and she tells me that she has been
seeing Orion wrong
when she points
to show me, i realize i have always seen
him upside-down, too

the right way around, he is
gigantic in the sky, his legs bent
as if to run, his bow pointed. it's
all a little much, and i almost miss
the slightly goofy, smaller version
of the slope-shouldered man i had seen

PORTRAIT OF A FARMER
November 20

Lung Ya in the field is
poetry in motion
a portrait of a solitary
farmer—advanced age,
bow-legged and slightly bent—
threshing rice with a
backdrop of blue sky and
mountains.

there are crabs in these
fields. tarantulas and snakes
and birds. Lung Ya knows
all of them, knows which
snakes not to worry over, knows
that crickets burrow and
make holes in the ground,
knows which plants will
survive being replanted
and which will not

the threshing is all blue and gold
behind his silhouette, raising the
rice above his head

*do you want another person
to help?* i asked.

no,
he told me that he has his own
way, his own rhythm, his
pattern. it is a luxury, i know,
to work at your own pace

to turn to watch the crabs scuttle
away, to smoke a cigar,
lean against a tree, let
the late-cut rice dry while you
thresh the early-cut rice. to make
it all into a picture that no one
else will disturb.

it is not usual
to work this way, not here, but
Lung Ya is an artist,
building and planting and
making the grains of rice fly in
their own arcs, watching them
fall.

LOVE FOR TREES
November 21

tamarind tree,
rubber tree
banana, rain
mango, teak
coconut palm.
i wonder
if i will love trees
the way God does
when i know all their names.
but God knows them
by heart name
by the landing and perching
of his own imagination—
all cells and strands of
DNA, waterways, capillaries

universes within

with a name i call you
and you may turn around.
i recognize and pluck you from the blur
of faces in a stream

but i do not have your cells memorized
i do not know your galaxies
i do not love you even a half fingernail
as much as God loves the pine,
cedar, acacia
or lemon tree.

LANGUAGE
November 22

i do not love the
Thai language because
it is beautiful —it is
more expressive than lovely
more vowel-happy than gentle.
i love it because
it is itself and it is here
in this place
where i have found myself
under the sky
amid bowing and hands
that meet gently,
just in front of the collarbone
or nose.

i love the rising
and falling, not from emotion
but scattered wildly
through every sentence
like potholes or sudden hills
i love the wide vowels and laughter,
the repeated words flickering
like lights that have welcomed me in

SCARS
November 23

i am not going to escape from this life
unscarred. i have blinked myself awake
and know
there is no *when this over,* there
is only love and trust—they bind
and we are not here forever, so
death or leaving come and the tearing
apart
well, maybe this is like trees. Jesus said
there is pruning.
sometimes the branches go up in flames
and certainly there are scars
tree sap running down the trunk of
the tree, trying to staunch the wound
and this is not the end of it. and yes,
it is worth it, yes i still think so.

A CALLING
November 24

    what can i say about the way the
    pandemic drags on and on
    news of a dark future
    hard days ahead.
    flights and visits are impossible
    and we are here by ourselves
    there are only a few of us now.
    it's still going
    mostly, honestly, it is okay
    we are together
    we are not sick
    there is the fear of lack of money
    alleviated by the rice in the barn
    bills that i stretch from day to day
    calculate which one i can pay
    the list of needs for sometime later
    grows and we pay
    a little there a little
    here
    and we talk about what we can
    and can't do
    in the most positive
    ways, like *we are learning how*
    to be resilient!
    honestly this lack is not
    necessarily from the pandemic
    these things just coincide
    come in clusters
    and i have been here before.
    i write it because a year of
    poems would not be complete
    without the breathlessness of need

shame and gratitude intertwined
especially in the night hours.
it is true, we are resilient
we don't stop growing
even in the most trying times
i remember being alone.
i remember trying to
make every birthday special,
each Christmas, until it became
a calling,
resilience,
a calling.

STARTED
November 25

the man next to me on the plane
is nodding off. there is a single
square of sunlight on his hand
from the window beside him
out there, the towns cluster
around the rivers, seeking water
the air is bright with light particles
dust and some other indescribable
glitter. my friend is on my other side.
earlier she pointed out that
the man's sweatshirt has
a single red word on the front:
started.

SWIMMING IN GOLD
November 26

i swam in the sea in reflected golden light,
light all around me, the warm sea, the
mountain in the distance. coconut trees
and kids playing on the shore. met forests of
seaweed under the water. *hello, hello,
oh dear, this is quite tangly.* the pier and
a long line of shacks, birds overhead.
rest and the light, like swimming in gold.

MAKING OUR WAY SOMEWHERE
November 27

my friend Ro talks to each cat
or dog she meets.
for a long time, really,
for a long time.
asking about
their days, scratching that spot
under their chins
or on their tummies. we move
slowly greeting each one
walking somewhere
maybe we are going somewhere?
maybe we are just making
friends with the animals in the corners
of every restaurant or alley
under the tables
at the counters where we
buy our things, waiting outside the
shops, heaped on chairs.
this is Thailand.
every block has dogs and cats.
we make our way
without rush,
my friend making friends
everywhere.

LITURGY
November 28

at the surface, we were like
fish, ourselves

i stretched my arms overhead
flying in a happy dream where

i belonged here.
hello, hello
for hours, floating

the other travelers did not seem to be
as entranced as we were,

i was in a constant state of
worship

praise thee, praise!
you made the large yellow fish
the small striped ones,
you made the coral
this underwater universe

it takes trust to remember you can breathe
the waves batted me up against
the rocks

like the most beautiful city
light illuminating depths and curves
and colors

i looked over at her
you made my friend, too

masked and flippered
surrounded by fish,
they greeted her, all around her
she floated near the surface,
laughing
at them

the blue fish,
the striped fish came close to greet us

hello
hello

swimming over and under our legs
right up to our masks

hello
hello
praise!

WAKING
November 29

      i wake in the dark
      and watch the stars slowly fade
      sometimes the moon is out,
      always i have coffee
      in hand.
      i am cocooned in words
      and thoughts.
      i allow myself to drift.
      the horizon grows pink
      the day is coming
      the day is coming
      and all the talking and
      socializing of the
      light.

THE BIRDS AT THE POOL
November 30

there were so many
swallows at the pool.
we sat and watched them diving
they came in sets
dipping to scoop water into
their beaks
the beach in the distance
the pier. these birds
small and neat, dipping for
a moment, just a little touch
flying by, just a
second, intent, brief,
graceful swooping.
and then up, away,
and circling back.
at the right angle, it looked
as though they were coming
right for me. i was in that
water, too, but i didn't dip
and drink.

DECEMBER 2020

MAYBE TODAY
December 1

there was another day,
—with the chipmunk.
maybe this trip seems
like it was all about animals.
i think it was.
yes, about animals and how thankful
we were, for God's love
shown to us through them
the simplicity
i was thinking about Advent,
about the waiting, and this
chipmunk was right there
right by the outdoor shower
at the pool

i get so tangled up in longing
so breathless that i freeze
at the question, *what do you want?*
if i were Bartimaeus, i would not have
known what to say—it is too fathomless
to look at. i both want too little
and too much.

the chipmunk explored
looking for something to eat
expectantly

he sniffed all around us.

Ro was in bliss.
i kept going back to my book
but she kept calling me to look

in a loud whisper
as the chipmunk searched her shoes
her bag, an empty
orange peel
the space under her elbow.
then he came to me, his
paws right on my belly
eyes scanning, nose quivering.

it seemed that he knew what
he wanted. that he was
thinking
maybe today will have
good things,
maybe there will be treats.

SMALL GLIMPSES
December 2

last scenes,
small glimpses
of the days on that island:
a restaurant in the house of
an older woman
with nineteen pictures of
the late King Rama IV
hung on her walls
alongside some posters of kittens.
some of the best portraits were there
the royal couple looking young and
gorgeous in sunglasses, the king
and his dogs.

in the background,
the woman's husband watched
muay thai, and the reedy sound
of the *pi chaawaa* floated around
the space
the food was so spicy.
we ate and drove home through
the flower-scented night

other things. the neat coconut frond
roof of the beach massage hut
and the woman there who gave
good advice about eating chillies and
bitter vegetables. *they are medicine!*
she told us.
the other woman who had eleven dogs
at home, all rescues, and more that she
fed on the beach. *they know the sound*

of her motorbike, the first woman
said.

the time we heard shrieking
and came around a corner to see
two men with a drone and a dozen
children jumping, trying to catch it
beside themselves with
excitement.

that night we were invited to a
party, but we didn't go
sunrises every day
breakfast. swimming
all the walks i took in the jungle
the long journey home by boat and
songtaew, plane, and car.
the feeling of resilience, of strength
returning.

ARRIVAL
December 3

      i barely got in the gate
      before
      the dogs were there to
      greet me
      and then the boys
      tore over to me and
      hugged me.
      Leafy, Solo, and Isaac,
      tall and without hesitation,
      we stood there
      arms around each other
      for a long time
      my heart swelled and broke
      with love
      oh, to have
      my arms full of sons.

I REMEMBER THEM
December 4

this rose
which starts out yellow
and then turns pink
slowly, from the tips
of the petals
like light touches of
watercolor spreading,
pinking up with oxygen
like a newborn
i remember them all,
the way their first cries sounded
the way they blinked or
kept their eyes closed
the smell of their breath
like roses
this rose
seems as though it can't
exist, breathing,
too perfect to be real.

THINGS I DO TO GET OUT OF WRITING MY DAILY WORDS:
December 5

light a candle
light another candle
light incense
check the news (maybe something good has happened? no.)
check my bank account (good surprises? no.)
get another cup of tea
rearrange the books on my desk
think of something to research
go to the Internet
forget what it was i was looking up
resurface twenty minutes later from
power washer nozzle searches
pick the roses i can see through my window
hug Isaac when he comes to my studio
smell the redwood cones in the jar on my desk
play with the pebbles in a jar on my desk
write a to-do list
plan new books
decide it's time for breakfast
wash five dishes
put the bread in the oven
draw on my open journal page
scroll through social media
jump up then sit back down
create writing playlists
dream.

LUNG YA
December 6

this time it is Lung Ya in the plants.
(Lung (Loong) means uncle.)
he has climbed directly into the thicket
of tropical sheaves—something like
a bird of paradise, but more so—
and his hat gleams out at me.
i can see him from the window where i write.
Lung Ya has lived here all his life
what a strange specimen i must seem
to him, following him with my phone
to get a good shot.
he wears a rust-colored
fedora when he's gardening. we have our
daily chats about compost and who could be
eating the kale (chickens, we think, but i
don't have the heart to turn them away.)
why didn't the basil come up?
neither of us know. Lung Ya
is slightly suspicious of my
gardening methods—his own are more
orderly—and fair enough. but some
things he admires. compost, for example
he cheerfully gets into the decomposition of
everything—the way it all falls into itself
and becomes
something magical, not ashes, not smoke
but rich earth. we spread it everywhere
and the roses bloom madly, and if i follow
Lung Ya, clicking away because he has climbed
right into the plants, he doesn't seem to mind.

THE QUIET
December 7

    the waiting happens in the dark
    and lately i find myself
    walking under a black sky,
    setting out when twilight is just beginning
    to purple the sky
    stars emerging like lit candles
    i avoid the dogs, carry a stick.
    the hill is so steep and i breathe in the
    cold air. i am waiting and waiting
    learning about loneliness, learning the solitude
    of family life, of married life, finding
    that i am always walking here, by myself
    under a great black sky. i look for light coming
    from the windows of houses, shining into the dark
    i am skittering by like a leaf, alone in hope.
    i am in the advent, knowing i have chosen
    this. the quiet inside is deafening.

LONGING
December 8

    i don't know what to do with
my longing
what to do with the difference
the coiled springs in my feet.
longing pulls at my cheeks and chin
brings me skidding into the dawn
running down roads, peering
around every corner. maybe there!
great heaps of golden straw
cows in a field. a woman with a
gray streak in her hair
how can i do things a different way?
a little kid with ice cream on his chin
a blue wall. a dream of a train
how can i harness my soul to work and love?
it's a tumble and a dangerous one at
that—lacy grasses black against a coral sky
long walks in the wind,
a bit of smoke in the distance.
longing folds and unfolds inside me
crumpled and indignant.

OPEN VOICE
December 9

    are we the only people like us
sitting in a circle in this world, singing?
it seems possible. Chinua is our
choir director, and we are from
Canada and Australia
Peru and Spain
England and Uganda
Poland and the U.S.
—more than
These countries, i've left out many.
a little dog
barks when our notes get high
or when we don't pay attention to
her. we are learning songs for
Christmas and we are outdoors
the sunlight through the palms
crosses the floor once, twice
shadow and light. the red floor
i am singing with all my fullness
all my ache.
a little angry
sometimes, as i sing. why is
the world like this?
not like the singing
that is okay. but everything else.
find your note, my husband says
i try it, and he smiles
perfect, he tells me.
—a sunburst in my chest.

SOFT-EYED GLANCES
December 10

these soft-eyed
glances between us
are a warm circle of light
we sit close and ignore small things
nurture our affection like a baby
feed it bits of memory like seeds
sunflowers bending wild on
the sides of the highway
you and i in the car. always moving
talking, even if you find my words
annoying sometimes, even if i find
you critical, i see this: our affection
blooms in the wild fields, it overflows
ditches, leaning onto the road
nodding back at us gently
scattering seeds.

MASKS
December 11

a masked life. we
smile but can't see
each other. it means love
yes, love and respect
of course the people from
the mountains often find
ways to make their masks
beautiful, as they have their
clothes, their baby carriers
for all of their lives
i admire the old man at
the stationary store
he has come into town
in the back of a pickup after a
long dusty ride from his village
he has that mountain stillness.
he's wearing a mask made
of fabric with wildly blooming
pink roses, almost growing
they are so vivid
his eyes are smiling
as he buys paper
and pencils.

MY JOB
December 12

    my job as i understand it is to
    show up. also to try not to cry
    i am sort of okay at both of those things.
    ha, ha who am i kidding? i always cry
    the words come toward me. i know
    i am the mom, the one who listens and
    doesn't leap toward criticism as
    though it is a knife. there are no enemies
    here. listen with your heart, with the eyes
    behind your eyes. cook something good,
    be free with your hugs, show up.
    don't cry.

NOT ONE THING
December 13

    i can't really describe the conversation.
    it was just one of those lost things. i asked
    for our mattress (we left it in the other house)
    and she said she didn't have it anymore
    that someone had taken it.
    we went back and
    forth like that for awhile.

    i watched the light play outside my window.
    we were speaking Thai and there is always the
    possibility of misunderstanding.
    the boys kicked a ball around in the driveway.

    but why would they take my mattress?
    i asked. something didn't add up and it
    made everything seem a little fuzzy.
    you can have one of mine, she said.

    i realized then that she had given it away.
    i didn't want one of hers but i thanked her
    anyway. it came with us from California
    and i remember sitting on it, talking
    to my grandmother before she died.
    Chinua lost his down jacket the other day,
    it just flew out of the bike, lighter than air.
    Ian gave that to me, he said.
    we don't want to let go of any of it.
    not one thing.

    it's okay, i tell my landlady
    in the language
    i have learned here.
    the one we have is fine.

LISTENING
December 14

walking in the dark
again
listening to the cries of
night birds—
owls and lapwings.
i cannot see anything
ahead of me
cannot see the path
feel it with my feet
my heart
listen to my friends
the birds
as they try to call to me
tell me which way to turn
farther in, farther in
come into the trees.

THE MIDDLE PART
December 15

my Beloved comes to me
on soft feet in my dreams
all outlined in fire
eyes like wells
just right there, he is
right there. i have heard his
voice in the forests of my
childhood, in the moss and
fallen leaf piles
but now i see the scars
the shadows
the times we have both
believed in better
and been bent by sorrow

lose your life again
he says
take my hand

when i wake i am crying
nothing can take him from me
endless love pours into me
closer than my skin
but i swear i heard him here
in this very room

and i can't go back to the
middle part
the close distance
the waiting.

NIGHT
December 16

night is the softest time
the hills slumbering
unseen
tonight,
Saturn and Jupiter are so
close,
and bright,
with a thin fingernail
sliver of moon
cradling them below
i am on this planet
in a long field of planets
it is right to feel small.
the owls are calling
the crickets tell me of
small things in the grasses.

ADVENT
December 17

we light the candles
eighteen of them today
we need all the light
read the old stories
the kids wait for
chocolate and lean on my arms
my knees,
Isaac's head is on my shoulder
listening closely. we hear
the stories and the pain
see the childlike
drawings, hum a little
light into our hearts,
draw closer, draw closer.

TWO TREES
December 18

those days
when your ribs can't hold you
and your heart is wide open
every leaf, every mote of dust
tracing light behind your eyes.

two trees stand like sentinels
great angels over the valley
i see the world between them
the pink sky in the distance
the light is unbearable
the beauty so sharp

i don't know how i am still
standing.

i should fall to my knees.

THE FULLEST EXTENT
December 19

    this time, COVID came through
    the Myanmar border.
    Thai women who came back across
    the lines in the jungle,
    leaving the hotel where they
    had been part of the "entertainment"
    industry, the newspaper said.
    they will be punished by the fullest extent
    of the law, declared the government

    people railed against these
    women. *hookers brought COVID to us*
    they said. *they have betrayed us*

    i think of women
    desperate enough to work in
    another country, in a brothel, in
    a pandemic

    when sickness came,
    all around them, they kept working,
    but when the lockdown came—
    no more work. they
    started walking through the jungle to
    get home. their bodies, susceptible
    to a virus, betrayed them. they

    have been betrayed often

    by

    the fullest extent of the law.

TWENTY-TWO POEMS ON HOPE:

1. HOPE OF WHAT IS NEXT
December 20

when morning came,
the sun rose and i decided to
rise with it.
i have been naive and
i have
dragged my hopeful heart
across the dirt
like a toy on a string.
i can see that now
leafing through the
papers of the summer
behind us.
okay, what now, i ask
the sun, and the creator of the sun.
palms out.
what now?

2. HOPE OF A TINY FIRE
December 21

i start the drive with hope and dread:
the mall. a tiny fire
can i find gifts that show my love
and honor? that soothe the
ache of this year of loneliness
and loss? here are my hands
here are the fluorescent lights
here are the shops and the masks and the
people hurrying from store
to store. i drive three hours one way
three hours back. i find small things,
impossible to offer so much love
impossible to represent my willingness
to give.

in the end it is only a mall
a drive
another holiday
another tiny fire.

3. HOPE OF BREAKFAST
December 22

for me today
oat porridge
full of nuts and seeds
sweetened with honey
from an old rum bottle
chopped apples
scattered on top
golden with turmeric
from our community garden.

i love to eat
breakfast. many times i have
heard that i should stop
but
today hope says
that i am allowed
to eat breakfast
if i want to. any day
every day.
oat porridge with seeds
and fruit

such a small enormous thing
to be able to eat.

4. HOPE OF THE LOGOS
December 23

why is there so much
comfort in a poem?
a trail of words finding space
between travails
carving a walking path,
or adorning walls
close comfort and hope of a
pattern, something that wraps
and binds and makes
unfathomable things
reasonable.
i don't believe it is empty
comfort.

is this what God spoke into
the world? the Logos a poem
a pattern of love, a human
who swept clean the cluttered
inner rooms —*come with me*
where do you live?
come and see
poetry, meaning, falling like
leaves
in a shaft of sunlight
suddenly everything adjusts
everything makes sense
oil on the head and feet,
God speaks a poem
into the world and all is
forgiven, all is loved.

5. HOPE OF CHRISTMAS EVE AT SHEKINA GARDEN
December 24

in the morning, i harvested
kale and bok choy
from my garden
i walked away
with great armfuls of greens
i drove to a shop
to order fresh ground coconut.
on the way, i passed a field
with a few water buffalo
one had found a tiny pool to
lie in. he was muddy and blissful
and had a little bird friend
with a white eye—new to me.
i picked up the fresh coconut and bought
two large packs of masks for people
who might need them at the
Christmas celebration
we practiced our songs
i cooked large pots of
food, dancing around the stove with Ro,
who made three pots of chana masala,
tea, and endless other things.
she was a storm of giving.
we used biodegradable
plates to serve food, so people could
simply throw their dishes
in the compost pile.
we sang in a large circle,
bigger than we had expected. sometimes
hope comes like a surprise, in the
midst of planned things:
songs and stories and light.

it was so cold, but we brought the warmth
and little kids from a nearby village
danced while everyone cheered.
that too, was
unexpected. like the water buffalo
that i had not expected to see
on Christmas Eve in his little bowl
of mud, and the new bird,
and the way some people's faces
shone back at me while i read
the Christmas story.

6. HOPE OF FREEDOM
December 25

what freedom to wake up
and know the day will be full of small
tiny beautiful things.
crepes and whipped cream
unwrapping of presents, and yes
i will drive back and forth
wrap presents at an uncomfortable
speed, forget things and offer
help to people who have
forgotten things. but i will also
watch and revel in their joy.

7. HOPE OF CHANGE
December 26

    the photos all showed
    lines of people waiting to be tested
    with the
    gentle marks of *tanaka* on their
    faces—a gentle swoop of yellow
    color on each cheek. you could
    just see it above the mask
    a dab on the forehead.

    migrant workers

    some blockaded into
    their apartments with razor wire
    the scourge of the time
    carriers of the virus

    what does this have to do with hope?

    all of them were tested
    put into treatment, and maybe
    this will save the older people in
    their communities. maybe this will mean
    new light on their living situations,
    how crowded they are, how untenable.

    in the harshest places and times
    new light dawns,
    things change, life comes.

    you are loved, i tell the people in the photos,
    though they cannot hear,
    every hour of every day.

8. HOPE OF TALL MESSENGERS
December 27

Ms. Dickinson wrote of hope
as the "thing with feathers."
i have imagined a sparrow—
a tiny trembling thing.
but it is no longer tenable
for the feathers so be so soft
so unassuming, and i now am
looking for the hawk, the eagle.

or maybe a feathered dragon,
an enormous fire-breathing creature
who will blaze my heart back into
life. or angels, tall messengers who
sing. *light and fire! light and fire!*
come forward! believe!
the veil is thin like tissue,
the stars will sing.

i need hope to take me in its teeth
to shiver me to the bone
to recenter me after this burning.
here in the ashes my eyes scan for
wild hope, wild, unexpected hope.
like Ezekiel's cherubim
their wings rushing
can you hear their feathers sounding?
roaring
like the voice of God
when God speaks.

9. HOPE OF SEEING THE MARKET BABY
December 28

the market baby can walk now
run, even. she can *wai*, pressing her
chubby hands together and grinning
at me with all her teeth. she bows
her head, then wriggles to be let down.

she would like to run through the market
pulling things off the shelves.
i have seen her do it. her grandmother
has lost a lot of weight, chasing
this perfectly gorgeous little creature
around

the love of every neighbor's heart

sometimes she is napping in the back
of the store, and then i tiptoe past to
find coffee beans, sugar, dried noodles.

it is so nice to be familiar to her,
to see her face light up
the most gentle of gifts
on a shopping day.

10. HOPE OF BELONGING
December 29

coming to the end of the year

i know how many times i
have taken false hope from the
idea that i can do anything
like some computer-driven program
when in fact,
i am only one human
woman.

i remember my past and how i
have driven myself
i can choose differently now
i can swim into warmer waters
this is what a walk is to me
over the hills in soft evening,
this is a gentle way of being.

it makes me feel as though i belong.

and i see real human things
a group of boys playing *dakraw*
in the golden light of late afternoon
they kick a woven bamboo orb higher
and faster than you would think
possible. the hills are soft and shifting
colors, from green to red to purple in the
waning light. it is slightly hazy

when i arrive home,
i work on a giant jigsaw puzzle
my daughter slumps beside me,

head on her arms, needing to be close,
needing to sigh while someone asks her
gently what is wrong and teases
her ailments away.

i have no plans
other than to continue learning.

11. HOPE OF WOMEN
December 30

    we gathered at the hot springs
    to soak off the old year.
    women of many
    ages, from many different
    countries
    and continents. languages
    the water welcomed us
    warmed us
    soothed our aches
    we have been working
    so hard
    so many things have hurt us
    these months, these days
    a collection of tears
    and resilience.

    i am learning what it means
    to be a woman.

    i got out and looked back at the pool—
    concrete ledges, women lying
    along the edges
    or in the water
    leaning back on elbows
    skin a gradient from very light
    to very dark, lines and curves
    and eyes and aching souls
    and joy.
    my daughter was there too,
    her own long lines blending into
    the image before me

like a painting
of work and love
persistence
fierce joy
and
the hope of the future.

12. HOPE OF THE NEW YEAR
December 31

waiting for the turn
from one year to the next
we eat Ro's pumpkin soup
and bread at her house
we are wrapped in wool and fleece.

next to me, my friend washes
lettuce from her garden
it is dark and we sit
in the light of a bare bulb
hanging from a tree.
we pick mint from the stems
eat it whole, another friend
brings tofu, Ro's landlord is
roasting pork over the fire.

we do this every year.

boys who used to be babies
at these gatherings
wrestle in the grass, consistently
getting hurt and crying.
eventually, they fall asleep
mine are all awake, the size
of giants, talking for hours.

Neil sets off fireworks
until a grumpy neighbor asks
him to stop.
we speak a mixture of Thai and
English and draw closer to the fire
i keep looking at my phone to

see if i can go to bed soon—

i do this every year also
but last year there were more of us
here, last year we didn't speak
about rising COVID numbers in
hushed tones

the exercise is hope

Ro's landlord tells us of walking
to Chiang Mai on an old road
when he was a child
it took three days
he saw motorbikes
he slept on mountain ridges
there were no car roads to get through
he is an old man, short with a
big heart, poking the coals with
a stick, like a painting

we draw close to the new year
close to the fire in the warmth
my sons are near me, leaning on
my arms or legs

at midnight the fireworks start
i kiss Chinua with all the hope in my
heart.

JANUARY 2021

13. HOPE OF THE UNKNOWN
JANUARY 1

so much happened last year
to tell us that we don't know
anything

i felt the heavy
breath on my neck, the chasing of
the last thing that i knew, the clinging—
i decided to throw myself into
the unknown,
so glad i was flirting with it
so glad i have tried in fits and starts

to live in the pool of stars
awash in their glow

people have asked me for my
five year plan and when i showed them
my empty pockets, they shrugged
me
off

but here we are in the same boat
in a sea of stars

nothing but explosions in the distance
the small warm lights in our hands
all that creation power still flowing in our
veins. how many days in the unknown?
how many phone calls, words written?

i will learn to play the clarinet
maybe

i could lose my lips
or my hands so maybe not
and yet

here i am, surrounded by love,
now
and now
and
now

beside the home fire of friendship with God
resolve has stiffened me, the unknown has
softened me, i turn to the Trinity
ask them for more of everything, more
roosters crowing, more birds in the trees
more sunrises,
praise!

14. HOPE OF THE DOOR
January 2

    he sings
    and i sit
    and listen,
    a drink in my hand
    i am
    tucked in a corner
    my back to the wall
    the way i like and
    i am here to
    listen. around me
    candlelight
    and warm sound
    my husband has been
    singing all of his life
    and i can't remember
    a time before his voice
    was there to remind me
    of heaven
    beauty beyond
    sight, or plans, or the known world.

    he sings and
    i fly
    through space
    my feet leave the
    ground, i hear
    God's call toward love and awe.

    this is art, yes?

    a door,
    opening.

15. HOPE OF BEING SEEN
January 3

it was my father's birthday
and i called him in the hospital
we talked, the line was fuzzy,
we couldn't get the video to work

my dad told me that
a nurse came in before dawn
to take blood, and when he told
her his name and date of birth
(have to keep the blood
in the correct vials)

she sang Happy Birthday to him

it's good, the way there is often
someone there
when you can't be. waving a small
flag that says—i see you.

another nurse brought him
ice cream
Mom was alone at
home. Dad's heart rate came
back down to normal.
after he was discharged
they celebrated his birthday
together again.

their relief.

16. HOPE OF COMING OUT OF THE DESERT
JANUARY 4

what i think i know now
is that i have allowed
hope to struggle along
like plants in the dry season

i am trying to listen
to you, God

*you don't believe you
are loved. you still don't know
how radiant you are to me*

it's true. this is not the music
i hear each day. the music of love.
rather, i replay songs of mistakes

hope is
you looking at me
i am watered by your gaze

change me

has there ever been any morning
like this? can we find each other
here? in this world now?

you come to me dancing
calling me out of my desert,

everywhere you step, plants
leap up, flowers grow

*it's okay to be you, you are
what i wanted, look at you here,
striding out of the desert.*

17. HOPE OF THE FUTURE
JANUARY 5

i hope for
train days
clacking wheels and
tea men making their
rounds

sweet breeze through
the window, palms
in the distance
the smell of cashew flowers

i hope for boat days
i want the horizon,
endless and moving,
silver and green
flying fish
catching the light

i hope for long talks
restored comfort
whatever it is that we are
lacking somehow, this
essential ingredient
i miss it so much

i hope for all my children's
tomorrows, for jobs and
teas with clinking cups
and light in coffee shops,
papers and pens, ideas and books
creation,
safety, music

and the love, the deep Divine love
surrounding them,
in them

i hope for dancing,
for outdoors, for tents
for campfires and delicious food
i hope for art and books
for whatever this is to pass

for hope.

18. HOPE OF FRIENDS COMING TO VISIT
January 6

what gentle joy to clean the house for the arrival
of friends, a lift of the heart. to imagine
welcome, a connection from their hearts
to ours, a place of rest for some time.

i remember back to my own travel
in Northern California, where my beloved
friends pitched a tent for me under a tree.
they dragged a whole mattress and down
comforter inside. soft pillows
i woke up to the gentle rustle of oak leaves
and the lowing of cows
and gazed up at the trunk and branches
of the tree through the transparent mesh
tent roof. there was no greater bliss.

how to fathom that kind of welcome?

or the cool *ungan* of my friends in
Varanasi, India. a courtyard centered around
their mango tree. (there are always trees
in these stories. always.)
cups of tea in our hands
i rifled through their library which
seemed to be comprised entirely of joy
i bloomed with rest

so on this day with every instruction
i say, *we want to make it nice for them.*
we want them to arrive, to sigh
to sit,
to breathe in welcome.

19. HOPE OF THE FLAME
January 7

i wake and blink the
night fear away,
bring my fire
gently
cupped in my palms
to a larger flame.
here:
feed mine with
endless fuel
let me hold it close
to my heart, let me
warm myself
my conversation and
movements, my touch, my
actions—
let them warm
others, draw them
near to the light and warmth
of this blaze.

20. HOPE OF CHILDREN
January 8

kids in the hot pools
showing their strength
warmed by
water that comes straight
out of the earth

kids in the rice fields
making forts or portals
a pathway through bushes
to another land

talking, jumping, crying
drawing, listening to one
another's stories

i have been surrounded
by children for half
my life

the confidante and supporter
of small people
with big worlds.

21. HOPE OF RESCUE
January 9

oh Holy One,
i have seen the signs
that people held
in the Capitol
as they violently smashed
their way
in

your name, Oh Lord
jarring in that place
with those angry eyes and faces

i have gritted my teeth
in response

you have bent very low
to kiss the forehead
of the frightened

where were you?
you were not in the
bulging eyes or the roaring
mouths, you were
in the back hallway

leading people away,
you were in the
hiding place.

HOPE OF THE LIGHT
January 10

hope is
the holiest of handfuls
no matter the darkness
outside, our hands
are full of this light

we will not give in
to the howling waste
we can't tell you how
morning will come

it is beyond us
you can sink into this
warm place
you can close your eyes

all around you,
light
sunrise
all around you, memory
of good things

it will hurt you if you
hold on

you will want to let go—

don't.

FULL-HEARTED
January 11

change is coming
and i hold my breath
in anticipation—the
different air in the morning
the new thoughts the
sounds i have not heard
for a long while. change
is not bad but it
always tickles at me like
possible grief. how
will i learn to run toward
it, full-hearted and free?

THE RETURN
January 12

all day we prepare
for the return of our friends
after a long pandemic
separation.
we wash sheets and
wipe surfaces, put duvet
covers back on.
they have finally flown
over the sea, stayed
in a hotel room for
weeks while people in
protective suits sent up
unimaginative food.
we want buckets of
flowers for them. we want
them to walk into light
and warmth, our welcoming
arms. this is a small
victorious thing. this is a
reunion. we have missed
them and they are
coming home
to us.

SO MUCH TIME
January 13

    we waited all day
    for news and sometime
    in the afternoon, heard the
    car pull in. we waved
    from the gate, then drew even
    closer, not sure if they needed
    to quarantine again.
    we stood in the street and
    smiled at one another.
    all the kids taller,
    so much time has passed.
    but somehow we are the same.

    homecoming.

REUNION
January 14

    i had worried,
    just a bit,
    that maybe they would feel
    awkward.
    Isaac and Jasper,
    friends since they were babies
    they like to tell the story of
    when they met, but can never
    quite recall when that was.
    ten months had passed since
    they last saw each other
    with so many new things
    happening in between.
    now they are taller, leaner,
    more thoughtful.
    but Isaac left our house
    immediately
    to sit on the
    street outside the fence, with
    Jasper and Elkie
    sitting on the ground
    on the other side.
    (we were waiting for news of
    a second quarantine—would
    the village leaders say they needed
    to isolate again?)
    all day, he sat there on the street,
    running home only to pack meals
    and school books to bring back.
    the neighbor
    had been burning bamboo leaves
    on the sides of the road—

there were ashes and when Isaac
came home he was covered
in ashes and soot,
from sitting on the street
in a pile of ashes, never happier.

I WOULDN'T EITHER
January 15

these days have been
so unsettling that my eyes
are tired from their ceaseless
scrolling. fires and tiny explosions
people losing their minds and
screaming. broken glass
the stories come out. what will we
tell the children? it has been
a rough year to be a teenager
i have to say we haven't really
earned their trust. a large white
building all the way across the world,
at first, we laughed.
then it grew more serious
why did they show us only now?
the real hatred, the real intent
these people have not earned my
brother's trust
nor my father-in-law's belief
nor my husband's.
and all of us white people, oh, after
this heartbreaking year i have come
away with the feeling that i wouldn't
trust us
either.

THE ARGUMENT
January 16

the argument was about olive oil
— hard to believe.
i won't repeat the details. it took
up more time than it should have
we don't have time
for trivial fights, we should
be feeding each other delicacies
or reading poems, listening to
piano sounds, watching clouds
tell me about the stars, not the
smoking point of olive oil, and i
will listen to you, rather than
yelling that you know not of what
you speak.

GOOD WORK
January 17

this morning i woke with
a slight lift of the heart
after wandering in the valley.
i wrote my words, tidied
art supplies and cleaned shelves
in the workshop. we can
still do good work. i showed
Chinua some songs i have
loved. he hummed along and
we can still do good work.

REMEMBERING
January 18

in the afternoon i read aloud
to the younger kids about nomads
in the fertile crescent. we made tea
and ate snacks, curling up together
—this is how i like to learn.

Kenya, walking by, looked in
on us and smiled
i remember this,
she said with soft eyes
i loved it.
we would read together
we always had tea and snacks.

all the fumbling i did—
my younger self.
all my mistakes
and my daughter
remembers the warmth.

MORNING'S ADVICE
January 19

i wake after dreams of monsters
just as
quiet night slips past,
leaving
through the window.
the stars are still out.
they disappear one by one and
morning comes with broken chains
in hand. i watch as she
throws the chains off the side
of the world. she turns
to look at me.
they are gone, she says.

do not go searching for them
they do not belong in your dreams
or touching your skin.

you were made to be free.

GOOD THINGS: A LIST
January 20

* you are good
birthday king, i see it all,
you stretching from your infant self
to this young man before me
the bated breath of the
world waits for you
you make music and
learn strong kicks, you
see through lies
you make lists of good things
that fortify you
you are fifteen years old
and no one can define you
except for you, Leafy,
remember it

* our friends came home
and Isaac has become incandescent
with joy

* we will watch the
new president's speech
and it
will not be hateful

* women are
wonders

* i am allowed to be

* the dogs are always
comforting

* green is a soothing
color and there is cauliflower
growing in our garden
i will eat vegetables today

* God has not given up on us
and

* we
have
each other.

AFTER SO LONG
January 21

how can it be that we are
in the house together
after so long?

i came here for months
like a ghost
pounded dusty sheets,
opened windows
how did the stray cats
get it? feral hisses
dry as a bone

we unplugged the fridge
turned the power off

but now they are home and
everything is alive, light has
opened up the rooms
we drink cups of water
eat curries and spring rolls

the kids are shrieking with joy
on the trampoline

reunion—it was so long

but it was not forever

AT THE BIRTHDAY PARTY
January 22

Chinua told ghost stories that
made the kids clutch each other.
their faces were
glowing in the firelight—
i don't think i've
seen anything lovelier.
i'm full of hope, today,
for Leafy and his life

the way he says thank you,
the way he includes everyone
this year has not been easy

but here he is at the fire
throwing jokes, his perfect teeth—
a genetic miracle—
flashing white in the darkness
his beautiful smile

we sang to him
i forgot birthday candles again
but it was okay because

we sang
and we loved him
and he knew it.

CARE
January 23

    i cooked leeks in water
    with a little salt, made broth
    with miso paste and ginger

    carried cups of this around
    with me all day. too much
    campfire smoke and late night talking

    i need water and soup and rest
    like a plant needs care, or a child
    or a mother who has
    worked hard
    and needs love.

AFTER THE CAMPOUT
January 24

after the campout,
the teen boys climbed out of their tents
in the hazy cold.
i could see them
crossing the lawn to get to the
house, i hoped they were warm in the night.
i was warm. i woke in the dark in my bed,
then came out and saw a few stars.
i moved softly so as not to wake
them, came inside to write
until the light came over the hills.

THE MARKET BABY RUNNING
January 25

yesterday the market baby
was running down the aisles
chewing on a piece of tamarind
whole, pieces of shell between
her lips. running,
she bumped her head on the edge
of a market stall and
wailed. three aunties surrounded
her, laughing and cooing, then
handed her to her grandmother.

comforted, she stood again. i
played with her, cocking my head
and turning in circles and she
grinned and did it back to me.

she has had a haircut, her
black bangs short across her
forehead. her face is nearly
perfectly round.

someone handed her a squishy
toy and she bit it. it burst and showered
tiny foam dots on her mother, grandmother
and uncle. they laughed
you bit it, what? they said.

no anger.

i touched her cheek and she
reached out to the nearest
vegetable pile, found a pea pod
and stuffed it in her mouth.

DELTA VARIANT
January 26

i watered all through the day
moving the sprinkler
again we're in the dry season
the grass crunches underfoot
leaves dropping or gusting
in a sudden breeze

the season of the koel
or the owl that
accompanies the morning dark
a coucal lives nearby with
his deep husky whoop

and i hate this virus

the line of the mountains is
faint now, the moon gentle
in the pink evening. we
continue

a bit bewildered

tending the things we
need to tend.

PAUL DEVENISH
January 27

my grandfather died yesterday
or today—

time is funny between
these hemispheres

and now he is beyond time

radiant
and powerful
again

he was a kind man
and a good one
in this life.

we lose things
and people
we do, this was something my
grandpa felt
and knew and

his Bible, so well used.
his voice in prayer. hands
preparing meals,
faithfully

face breaking open in a
ready smile, this father of my
father, i feel his

gravity in my life
the offering of love
he planted

it never let me
go.

GOOD WOMEN
January 28

on the phone
my dad told me that
the social worker
had looked in on
Grandpa throughout
his last day

and she saw
the nurses
there, stroking his face
running their hands
through his hair

comforting him
these good women who knew
him in his last days

their kindness

their hands on his head
blessing him

as he headed
home,
known and loved.

FIRST HUG
January 29

and here now is
Isaac, son of laughter
hugging me
one arm slung around
my shoulders—if i have
done nothing else today
i have looked into his face
and smiled my delight
into his eyes.

Isaac the youngest
the dancer, the one who loves
numbers and playing with their
connections and clicks,
rubbing them together
like marbles

eight years of joy
with this last baby
the son of laughter
who walks down
the short hill to find me
in my studio, my first
hug of the day.

LIKE WATER
January 30

in the morning,
koels. i hold my grief
in my hands like water.
i don't know where to put
it, cannot form a thought
or sentence to clear the

it is like walking through
one cobweb after another
never quite

but the birds are calling
in the distance even though
i am disappointed in myself
again, even though my
eyes cannot

owls and koels
morning companions
one lit candle
how can i

RAIN
January 31

    yesterday it
    rained, the second day
    in a row. a gift!
    dust rose up
    the first night, the scent
    of the spores making their
    way into my dreams,
    we all woke to look at
    the opening sky.

    the water brought
    something to the surface
    in the rice paddies, something
    tempting to the white egrets
    who landed to snack
    there

    what we receive is too
    great for our hearts, a fresh
    sky, the line of mountains visible
    again, the birds who grace us
    with their gentle
    presence.

    i have been so sad
    and yet joy breaks in
    again and again.

FEBRUARY 2021

TWO WILD WOMEN
February 1

who are we, then?
two wild women on our old
rattly motorbike,
mother and daughter
seeking adventure
on roads through fields
and teak forests
in boulder-strewn pastures
while farmers in straw hats
finish their day of work
ready for dinner and rest.
how to get to the mountain
we wonder, to climb up
into its arms?
Kenya is on the back
of the bike
occasionally leaning forward
to give me impulsive hugs.
the fields are full of garlic
now, the whole world new
after the rain
there was another
power-cut in the storm
who knows when
the lights will be back?
but we don't care,
we are driving out
driving on dirt roads,
through villages,
the dogs watch us idly
not yet charged up for protection

in these early evening hours.
we let a farmer in a truck pass
and he laughs his thanks with
a gap-toothed grin. all is well.
all is completely well.

COMMUNITY LUNCH
February 2

there is Uma, from Korea, who longs for
India and makes jokes about the dogs
howling within her, or the way she
has nothing to say, but is so vivid, so
full of brilliance that she makes everything
around her dull,
and Faith, who is planning to move
back to Uganda, who told me stories of her
sister and mother, the way she grew up,
her dreams and plans for community
i will miss her so much when she is gone
there is Miki who tells us stories of growing
up in Catalan and Fina who is from
the kingdom of Brunei and traveled to
Africa to learn to play ngoni, and Sarah
from the snowy plains who loves to laugh
and Richard, her love, who fell off a mountain
in India and nearly died—he came away with
a whole new personality. there is Nokk who
lost her grandmother who raised her
in Isan where the days and food are hot
and Yo from Peru with half blue hair
Kayla with her son who is toddling into
everything, dropping pot lids while we chat
and Vincent who once was a
Quaker pastor and left to wander in India,
there is David, who is blunt and smart
and says too much, getting himself in
trouble, but is quick to apologize,
and Kenta from
Japan, Asura from Italy. i am forgetting people
and i don't know them all but—

look at these people who are sitting
and eating my food, drinking Winnie's chai
eating Ro's cake
look at Chinua playing guitar and Neil
dreaming, Joshua talking with someone
near the fishpond. look at the love
see how blessed we are.

THE CLIMB
February 3

a long walk up a staircase
past teak trees with fallen
leaves and spiraling crispy
seed pods. i breathe warm
eucalyptus fragrance.
every so often some
dry leaves come dancing up from
the ground in a pattern, like
they are alive—a tiny dust devil—
they lie back down before they can
do any damage. i push myself
to walk the steps without stopping
i nearly make it but i pause once,
twice. there is a large white Buddha at
the top and very little shade.
it is midday. i cover my head
with my hand and look out over
the valley, trying to piece it
together from the sky. i know the
other view, the face-front ribbon
building after building
and landmarks from the tiny height
of a person. it has always been
harder for me to see from above
and i find it all so surprising
those buildings are close to one another?
the river swings that way
curves so extravagantly?
three men climb the stairs as i leave.
i would stay longer
but i need to pick my sons up
from their language lesson.

the men wear long-sleeved shirts
they are panting and sweating.
i feel breezy and tall,
though as i walk down the steps,
my legs tremble.

OUT OF SLEEP
February 4

my dreams have not been
good for a long time now.
every morning i wake and have
to wrestle my way through
thorn bushes, the way
Chinua and i tussled with bushes
on the side of a hill in Dharamsala
that one time when we were
lost for hours, over twenty years
ago. i walk steadily
upward, force myself from the
warm bed. start the water for coffee.
why the heaviness? why the
sinking?

we walked for hours,
clambering over boulders in
a creek canyon, tired and shaking
when we finally spotted, in the distance
the lights of the town.

THE CABBAGE
February 5

the world pulls itself to pieces
in unease and fear
but, in the garden
the cabbage throws out leaves
sends life through veins in
colors you can't fathom
teal and dusky purple
soft mauve, gray.
the cabbage lives low to the ground
unfurling too slowly to see
building in sequence
layer upon layer
first the leaves, then this
protected heart, with pages
like many hands
closing over one another
fingers overlapping and enfolding
patting gently the center
the marvel, the soul.
the cabbage
does not ignore the rumors
of loss and lack
it knows about the feet of armies,
but its cells can only move in these
purpling waves, motion so soft it
uproots dynasties and soothes
the aching heart of the world.

THE GIFT
February 6

something like the peace
of shadows and light on a wall
or curtain, or leaves in a gentle
wind, or the morning's first
cup of tea—i want to give these
to you. that you would know
and know and know and know
the *ever-present help in time
of need*.
hold it close to you. or wait
for it to come thundering into
your camp, like the hooves of a
thousand horses.
you are not alone.

ONE STEP
February 7

i lie curled;
a puddle of a person
without much strength.
where is your agency?
where is your power?
i gave it away, too many
times, and now i don't know
how to retrieve it. where to
find it. in the garden?
at the page?
scattered in the grasses or hills?
do i hunt on hands and
knees? or look for it in the sky?
is it at the canvas, or in
my clarinet? i am often
frightened of myself, and alone.
maybe searching is too much
one muscle at a time
i lift myself from my hidden place
stretch and drink a glass
of water.
if i can take one step
it will have to be enough.

MONEY TALK
February 8

    we talk every evening
    about things that we want
    to share with them. tonight
    it is money. i have made mistakes
    and i tell them so they will
    not be fooled. remember the men
    at the car dealership?
    how they were so nice?
    it is not fair this
    world, but sometimes when
    people are nice, we have to ask
    questions.

    here, children, is what i know
    about currency: there is no easy money
    do not let it own you
    the way to keep the chains
    off : make sure there is always
    something you are giving away for free
    (welcome, we say every week,
    at Shekina. come in, have
    a plate of food, sit down, here is
    tea, there is nothing you need to offer,
    not even thanks)

    let people pay you, i tell the kids
    but then, to knock the whole thing
    down, to flip the tables, to enter
    the alternate kingdom,
    to trick the thing that
    would catch you in its web—

give things away!
give art to someone who cannot
afford a painting, give food,
give time.

THE THUNDER
February 9

the thunder woke me,
very aware of its own power,
its voice. the sound broke the sky.
it broke my sleep, my
tentative grasp on peace
i rolled along with it
and then the rain came and
it too wanted to shake us
from our beds, but we
burrowed farther in and i
felt the rasp of excitement
in my lungs, the readiness to
leap screaming into the storm.

SORROW
February 10

lately, every time i get quiet,
sorrow comes padding in
her feet cracked and calloused.
i distract her with lists and
trees and little boy hugs but
she prefers to lie in my chest
reclined, waiting for any silence
any chance to grip me
again. i will not be able to evade her
maybe i will learn, one day,
to let her sit at my hearth
let her sing over me
until she is ready to go off
into the night.

THE WORK OF A WOMAN IN THE MIDDLE OF HER LIFE
February 11

to tell a story
to be free
to live
to form a body of work
to wrestle with everything
she has been given and not been given
to resist the idea that
somewhere there is a more perfect
existence, a place to be known more fully

to be known here

to stay

to shape love like bread
and feed it to others
to trust and ache with loss
to grieve what was and
accept what is
to break through apathy and
keep the veil between spirit
and material thin
to read love in the sky, the
branches of trees and in the faces of
the people around her,
to be true to herself
to stop throwing herself away
to walk the shores of the ocean of
her loneliness
to come gently with friendship to her
her soul's warm hearth

to honor her sorrow
to claim a space for herself
in the solace of God's regard.

PRAYER
February 12

my heart is bent to the
earth,
i am low to the ground
i rest my ear on the grass
and hear beneath
me, the sighing of the rocks, their
groaning
come and heal us
they have stripped us bare
the worms in their tunnels
the ground crickets who make holes
i am crying, my heart melting down
arms spread,
come and heal us
come and save us

I DREAM OF BIRDING
February 13

last night, in my dream
we were birding, all of us
and everywhere, everywhere
there were birds.
all we had
to do was look, and there—
another one!
rare and colorful
on powerlines and in the eaves
of buildings. one had a lacy
long tail. one had a head made
of bright blue and green beads
strung together. one bright
beaded eye.
what is it? i asked in my dream.
a beaded barbet, the answer came.
it made perfect sense.
they were everywhere. we cried out
again and again at the wonder
all these birds
so close, right there.

NO GRAND CONCLUSIONS
FEBRUARY 14

i have no grand conclusions
about love— we are a work in
progress, moving through this drawing
and there are eraser marks everywhere
scribbles in the corners of the pages
i have taped more pieces of paper onto
the roads i marked up, and you
used your hands to fold shapes that
drew me to you, you were there in the
beginning and you are there now,
we are two solitudes
we are using charcoal with grand sweeping
arcs, we are painting with our hands.

MISPLACED
February 15

everything beautiful!
i draw these words in the dirt
sitting as i am in the dust
scattered leaves around me

almost afraid to believe

everything beautiful—the
daily work, the numbers,
the decisions
searching for clothes, cooking food
for the dogs
everything beautiful

my own heart
but

i have misplaced my hope

i will stitch tiny lines like the
ladies at the market, sew these tasks
together, you'll be there too, singing
over me. splashes of color, birds
calling from the bushes, flowers
in the rising sun

numbers carry their own beauty
even in the negative they cannot define
the shape of a person, the sigh and fall
of their hair or breath

i have made my own choices

the pond heron in my yard has barely
chosen, she has flown as though guided by
a light hand. she is beautiful

and a light and gentle hand
has guided me, has held out

everything beautiful.

THOUGH I DID NOT KNOW
February 16

      i danced— more than once
      three, four separate times today

      this body is mine after all
      it cannot go back
      though too often i try to force it.

      hand, where do you want to go?
      do you want to fly up?
      feet? do you want to pound
      into the earth, into the dust,
      on the grave of injustice, on the
      broken bars of all these cages?

      yes, under the trees
      yes, with the other women
      yes, to the drums inner thudding

      i feel it in my heart, my hands, my chest

      the women followed me
      though i did not know what i was doing
      and we danced.

A SMALL STUNNED THING
February 17

i fell
from a long height.
we were singing
and there had been
too many confusing
things in the past
days. i spend too
much time thinking.

so there, in that circle

well, our voices
poured out and my love
felt too frail to handle much
more and my heart

was a bird
rescued from the teeth
of a monster

alive, but stunned and shaken

i could not stop crying

the motorbike drove me away

the crying girl in the villages
up into the mountains
God held me in his palm
a small stunned thing
alive

YOU KNEW
February 18

i dreamed that my belly
was full of stars; a galaxy
swirled in my cells,
they moved out to my
fingertips, to my toes—
you see me and have made
me this way, you knew
what i would be, you
brought me here
to this world
this time, this motherhood
the stars in my veins
you see.

THE OLDER BROTHER
February 19

the older brother was afraid
that the younger would get

everything good
that there would be nothing left

that he would be unseen
and empty

(i am afraid
i have always been afraid)

but his father's voice was so soft
the son could hear
his heart drumming
in his chest
a song of love

all that i have has always been yours
all that i have
is yours

A CROWD
February 20

a crowd at my house
making candles
melting wax, waiting for the right
pouring temperature

riding bikes, running in and out
help us get ready for the party!
what should we bring?
where is my backpack?

i'm hungry
waiting for food
looking for a hug

at the birthday party
all these kids who have
grown up in this town

the virus is not here
in our mountain town

we can sit on the grass
watch the kids run by
looking for drinks
for hugs

hello, hello

i am here.

THE BOY THEY WAITED FOR
February 21

    my friend, Jo, tells me about
    how her son was born

    —we tried for many years, we got
    money from an inheritance
    my husband said, we need to
    do this, IVF—he was
    the first try—
    we didn't want to name him
    in the womb
    just waited
    holding our breath
    i had a crazy youth when i
    first came north from Bangkok
    you do this when
    you need freedom, but it cannot
    continue. he came. we couldn't
    believe it—

    while she speaks, the love spills
    over and he comes back again
    and again for a quick hug
    a kiss, the boy they waited for.

CAMPING TRIP
February 22

leaving is like pulling up tough roots
how do we exist outside these walls
and beams
surely this is not all that we are
slowly it comes together.

the bags, the tents, the blankets
and mats for the ground
the food and gas cylinder

last minute oil change
we drive into the mountains

i have been frantic
ready to flee

we arrive and find places to sleep
this part is always hard for me
wanting the best place

once the tents are in place
my heartbeat starts to slow
my cells rearrange themselves to
move with the sound of the river

the light changes and glows
we lie back
we put our heads to the earth
a gentle thudding, rushing

lulls us to sleep.

TWO SOLITUDES
FEBRUARY 23

it was the softest kind of day
spent outside in golden light
hot but only enough to relax
the muscles.

the water buffalo
crossed the stream and ate
with their bells clanging and we
watched. their birds walked
beside them, white and as
graceful as the buffalo were
clumsy. buffalo mouths, snatching
at leaves. it's enough to
bring tears to your eyes.

the hot, sulfuric water
the cold river

Rilke said that true love
is *two solitudes that
meet, protect, and greet
one another.*

that flash of white on the
back of the buffalo, a gentle
wing flap.
two solitudes. a soft touch.

the water, the sun, the faces
of friends. you sat on the tree
limb and played music

a perfect solitude. the white
birds against the sky, my heart
bordering, greeting yours.

ANOTHER GOODBYE
February 24

my friend, Faith, had to
leave the country suddenly.
she called me in the morning,
crying. her sister had passed away
unexpectedly
and she needed to book a flight.
could she donate some things?

i went to her house
and sat on the floor, we
looked each thing over.
she packed up her hula hoops
and fire toys, her roller skates.
she readied herself for the change.

these friends who have
been here through the year
of pandemic—they are
close now.
losing one feels like tearing
a plant from the earth.
and Faith, so beautiful
so kind. always storing up
things to tell me.

what was i going to tell you?
—oh yes!

she gave us the leftover
food from her pantry. a bottle
of apple cider vinegar. a nice
pepper grinder. Ro and Kenya

came over as well and
Faith showed us pictures
of her sister. of her mother

dusk fell. we could barely
pull ourselves away. in the morning
i saw her briefly, next to the fields
she had tears on her cheeks
my friend
i hugged her.

this was so sudden
another goodbye.

FOR US
February 25

we had a day of chores and
appointments, then
scooped Kai up and went
for dinner.
what makes a café?
Kenya asked. i looked around
at the cluster of tables, the
lanterns at the wall.
we ordered pizza in Thai.
the boys were playing
chess. a man wandered over
to show his baby the large pizza oven,
the flames, the wooden paddle
the happenings.
i remember doing the same with
Isaac when he was a baby, keeping
him happy while we waited for the
food.
our table was next to the street
and we could see the nearby temple
a monk in orange robes
took out the trash.
motorbikes went by
less frequently than usual.
these streets are quiet. for us, this
is a café.

LUMINESCENT
February 26

Ahmaud running
it was a little over a year ago,
though
that is hard to believe.
i want...
do you think i am going
on and on?
i want...
Ahmaud to run.
to run and to be left alone
for people to smile
as he goes, lift a hand

oh, Ahmaud, i am sorry.

my son runs barefoot
up and down our road
he is fifteen, but far taller
than me now. when Ahmaud
died, or when we heard about it
we ran for him.
i told my kids about the way he
died. this is not the world for them.
they are too luminescent for this
beast of history.

we did not know then
that the stories would keep
coming, we did not know
how blazing the truth would
be, how we would all be burned
into ashes last summer

the fire is good
and true, but the tinder
tears our hearts from our bodies.
you are too luminescent for this
world.

Ahmaud glowed when he ran.

THIS IS NOT FOOD
February 27

you were not made
to eat gossip as food
to live off of meager scrapings
of outrage and glee
to search opinions for lies
or hear one thousand takes.

oh, this life.

there was something more
than air in the air
yesterday —we

have you noticed yet,
how mean they can be?

mind your business.

there was something more than
air in the air
yesterday —we thought it was
golden. sparks danced around
us and we were transformed
the tables set as for a feast

we ate love we drank peace

these filled us.

PRAYERS FOR RAIN
February 28

that haze
life has turned again
and the sky is covered over

our hearts hold a glow
that cannot be extinguished
not even by skies
full of smoke

we sang out our grief
thumping the floor
singing from our bellies
singing with crackling throats

our little circle
so lovely

then the song turned
as songs do
into prayers for rain
calls and cries

we sang
through that haze
the glow in our hearts
like blue
like water
like the beauty that
we cannot yet see.

MARCH 2021

CIRCLES AND CIRCLES
March 1

this month changed
everything last year
and yet at this time
we still didn't know

all the cracks that
would open beneath us
and we didn't know that
we would wonder if
we could survive

and that we would
muster every bit of
strength and go on.

OUR PLANS
March 2

    i remember
    looking at
    our plans
    —a trip to Vietnam
    we wondered
    should we go?

    what would the
    safe thing be?

    whispered conversations
    in the kitchen

    we came so close to the
    edge of that precipice.

    how carefully
    we stepped back.

WE WILL BE
March 3

this softness
we are
rebuilding the walls
of this house
side by side
nothing is more
worth it. your arms
beside mine, your
laughter

we have been
the two of us

we will be
the two of us.

ABSCONDED
March 4

>i fell and pressed my
>face to the fallen leaves
>the dry grass
>
>absconded, the message said
>
>we prayed with everything
>we had, barely daring to move
>
>we asked for a steady
>footfall, arms outstretched
>we asked for protection
>
>how had the doors failed?
>it didn't seem real
>
>we prayed with desperation
>our mouths making tiny sounds
>from so far away
>
>a sudden wind, like a desert
>clearing, leaves rained down
>on us, on my back and in my hair
>
>it roared around us
>i felt heard, felt the power
>
>a few minutes later, the text:
>
>found!
>
>tears and trembling limbs
>and deep gratitude

SHAKE
March 5

do things a new way
empty the shelf
rather than
fill it
bring the open basket

wait for fruit to fall

shake the tree
shake the house
shake limbs and soul
move some way
flail your arms your legs
who cares who sees

do things a different way

mouths hungry and open
all around you

hands open

you can't hesitate— this is
too much too important
we're ready for you now

break the walls
come close and listen—
you can be whoever
you can burst out.

I MEET A FRIEND
March 6

it happens sometimes
in this town, that i meet
a friend in the store
having a hard time
buying their groceries
wandering and finding
nothing or everything
teary-eyed and lost.

i am offered
these confidences
how is it that life can
be so tender and so hard?

we talk for minutes
and hours and maybe the
shop proprietors are
confused about these
long talks in aisles
the way we seem
to go nowhere

to offer solace in
unexpected sections
of the store, by the bread,
with the teas.

THE SKY WILL COME BACK
March 7

this will pass

i will not remember the
taste of ashes

the sky will come back
to us, we will remember

blue!

hold tight,
ashes in our eyes
i stop and blink them out

blue! i remember it

we all sang together
there were so many
different colors of joy
i was not dried out

like an old leaf

i walked the hills

i remember

THE CARETAKER
March 8

at community lunch
the migraine made me
fuzzy around the edges
sick to my stomach
and i almost went home
but stayed talking

with a friend

such deep revelations
i grew up in an orphanage,
he told me

words dropped right there
among the trees, beside
the workshop, to the tune
of the saws.

so much story there
a way of being
life and questions and need
loss and sorrow

i never get used to being
the caretaker
of this sharing

WHICH PART?
March 9

which part of the body holds the
belovedness? it seems that it
must not be the arms, hands,
or legs. especially not the feet,
though these are all, in fact,
beloved.

beloved as the sky
the moon, the stars
that sing back down to me.

but these are the doing parts
the working and holding and
typing, chopping, walking for
hours and hours parts. the
standing, making, sweeping

what i am saying is that
i am not going to believe that
i am beloved because of my
hands.

they do not hold it
is it the heart? the brain?
all still so functional
where does the belovedness live?

also not in the gauziness
of strength, the slipping away
nature of grit, the falling down
propensities of joy.

these are all good things, but
they do not hold it. if i lose them
i do not lose my belovedness,
dear one. neither do you.

maybe in the air between air
whatever part of my soul remains
waiting, the part that knows its
home. the space between cells
the million circuits that reach toward
their God, the memories of being
attached, like an umbilical cord, like
curling up and breathing the heartbeat
of the Maker.

it is
in being.
it is in being held.

WRITE WHAT YOU WANT
March 10

write what you want
your home to be and
how you want to walk
through the world, and
what eyes you want to
use and how you want
to look.

write it
write your soul
and soothe the
hurt places
like gentle cleaning
with a soft cloth

don't examine
like a doctor, but maybe
like a mother,
do you need a sleep?
a snack? a bath?

write art
write your relationship with God
draw this with lines
that don't really make sense
except to you
and maybe a few others
who need to see it now

live in poems

leave the rational space
is there a word for this?
enter dreams.

YOU WOULD BE MORE CAREFUL
March 11

i don't think you know who we are

if you did,
you would not dare
touch us

Breonna, Sarah, Chelsea

not your daughters
your sisters
yours

we are the singing heart
of the part of God
that curls around
a precious seed
breathes it to life
we are strokes of beauty
outlined in light, we are
breath and strength
lionesses, we are waiting
for a day when you will know
we are God's own

and i feel

worried for you
you have messed with
something mightier than
you were ready to comprehend
you have dared to try to
possess something that

was never yours
still is not yours
to touch
or take.

you are not ready for
the returning
rush of flame.

ON THE WAY
March 12

    we are on the way
    to get braces for my
    girl— the first time—
    and the car is filled
    with music because we
    both love driving with
    songs surrounding us
    like the light
    through the trees
    we exclaim over the same
    things.

    we are also different
    i never had braces

    never lived in a pandemic
    as a teenager

    never made art
    like hers

    i love our two faces, though,
    aimed at the sun
    at the moving light
    the leaves, the mountains,
    the lines of things, the
    way they stir
    within us.

TODAY, FOREVER
March 13

Kai in my heart
today,
forever,
Kai
in my heart forever
my tall son
with his long hands
and brilliant smile

the boy who traveled with
us into the second year
of our marriage
and then across the
country into rivers
and hot springs
and lakes
always there
with his eyes and his
smile
questions, ideas
constant motion
little dances

this year has not been
easy on my boy

would i rewind, if i could?
i don't know,
i don't know,

what a question you ask

who can know what future
brilliance would be lost
if we had not had the pain

i want him to be
himself
to be deeply held
to know himself loved.

IT GROWS
March 14

    real love goes beyond
    in constant motion—it stretches
    grows, shifts like light, dances

    it even moves toward the past
    soothing the ache, enveloping
    every lonely moment
    in kindness.

    love looks at the offerings of
    flowers and leaves, the tiny homes
    built in ravines and on hillsides
    and murmurs, thank you

    love sings peace over your
    confusion

    love sees your messy hair
    and your snaggle teeth, love is
    moving outward to your neighbors
    to the mountains, the powwows
    to school, to the
    girl with epilepsy you guarded
    because the teachers asked you to.
    you were only eight but they
    knew you had the love

    love makes you cry for the boy
    who came back to the school to
    demand his knife back from the
    teacher who took it from him
    —*my dad gave me that knife!*

love lived with the kids on the edge,
the Polish kid with the leather jacket
and the accent
your beautiful transitioning friend
the girls, who like you, stood waiting
on the outskirts of the dance
the girls with a reputation
the farm kids
the punks
the refugee kids
the pregnant teenagers
the tallest and shortest

you hovered you hovered
feeling this love
touching down every once in a while
but it was often unbearable
you wrestled
you were all on the precipice

but love was always moving
folding you in.

COUPLE ON A MOTORBIKE
MARCH 15

    i was driving behind you
    i was a stranger
    you were on the back
    of the motorbike

    a white bow in your hair

    the late afternoon sunshine
    turned you to gold
    wind in your hair
    your clothes

    driving on the flats
    fields of cows and water buffalo
    the sun on your face
    the white bow catching the sun

    i don't know you

    when i passed you
    i looked in my mirror and saw
    your companion,
    the breeze moved his collar

    the two of you so beautiful
    so young
    red motorbike, his shirt flying
    across his collarbone

    both of you outlined in light

WHAT YOU SAID
March 16

what you said is true
i have imagined myself
solitary in responsibility
for an eon
a heron in the field
you have caught me up
in a swirl of white birds
and i insisted there was
no one else around

everyone has their shell

i have never quite
known how to be in the
swirl, rather than insisting
on solitude with tight-fisted
hands

you know this about me

i can feel your heartbeat
though i am afraid.

LIKE A STAR
March 17

seven of us
from five different countries
lay on the floor like a star
our heads at the center
feet out
looking up at the grass roof

i don't even know who
started singing first
it was effortless

how many moments passed
while we made the song?
we didn't care who heard us

what an unexpected
shelter, such an
open-handed gift.

THREE WORDS
March 18

with his resonant voice
he gave me three words
brave
generous
and powerful
and i was surprised
by each one.

THE MARKET BABY LAUGHING
March 19

under this high metal ceiling
the air is hot and still,
smoked with the season's
air
the vegetables are
wilting,
the vendors wiping at
their foreheads
but
the market baby has energy
and no time for greetings.
she is power on
short chubby legs
racing away from her grandmother
grabbing at mushrooms
no no no no no no
who taught her no?

teeth flashing

laughing and falling
i buy tofu and tomatoes
as many as i can fit in my
bag
when i am nearly done,
in the back of the shop,
the market baby is curled
up on their mat on the ground
tucked into the c-curve of her mother
quiet now,
lashes drifting downward.

ACKNOWLEDGMENTS

I want to thank every member of my Wild Seeds Patreon group for this book. This is the safe little space where I published all these poems, freely and immediately out of my head. They still get my daily poetry and like it, and they encouraged me to go on. They were my companions as I wrote the poems during this year.

Thank you Julie Reinhardt, Alison Hake, Christina Jordan, Mary Hall, Gale Mosgofian, D Dun, Kimberly Powell, Bob Kohlbacher, Carrien Blue, Trisha Devenish (Mom), Meggan Hayward, Anne, Wenda Friesner, Julie Winslow, Gretchen Spiro, Anja, Lora, Bec and Nick, Anita Yoder, Eva Edens, Amanda Friese, Jacqueline Murray, LeeAnn Scovel, Jemma Allen, Tracy Harris, Karen Engel, Teresa Q, Rose Anderson, Jessie Benkert, Elisha Pettit, Annie Laurie Nichols, Kathleen Andersen, Alicia Wiggins, Diane Brodeur, Erin Smith, Ro Keyzer, and Sue Kauffman.

You are truly the best, most encouraging readers in the world.

Thank you Chinua, for encouraging my poetry from the beginning. Thanks also to my daughter, Kenya, for being such a lover of words, to Leafy, Solo, and Isaac, who are proud of me, and to Kai, who every once in a while stuns me by calling me a professional. Thanks to my mom and dad, you are so wonderful. Thanks to my brother, Ethagbhe for telling me your stories. Thank you Becca for inspiring me with your whimsy. Thank you Leaf for calling me a poet, and thank you Ro for being a partner in crime. Thank you Faith, for your friendship.

Thanks Neil and Aya for long talks, and Naomi and Josh for coming home halfway through the year and bringing light into our lives. Thanks, Elkie and Jasper for being the best fans. Thanks for all those who told me their stories or briefly touched my life. You are so beautiful.

ABOUT THE AUTHOR

Newsletter

If you want to join Rachel Devenish Ford's newsletter and learn about books and new releases, sign up here. Your address will never be shared!

~

Bio

Rachel Devenish Ford is the wife of one Superstar Husband and the mother of five incredible children. Originally from British Columbia, Canada, she currently lives in Northern Thailand, inhaling books, morning air, and seasonal fruit.

~

Works by Rachel Devenish Ford:

The Eve Tree
  A Traveler's Guide to Belonging
  Trees Tall As Mountains: The Journey Mama Writings- Book One
  Oceans Bright With Stars: The Journey Mama Writings Book Two
  A Home as Wide as the Earth: The Journey Mama Writings: Book Three
  World Whisperer : World Whisperer Book 1
  Guardian of Dawn : World Whisperer Book 2
  Shaper's Daughter: World Whisperer Book 3
  Demon's Arrow: World Whisperer Book 4
  Beloved Night: World Whisperer Book 5

Crown of Stars: World Whisperer Book 6
Azariyah: A World Whisperer Novella

Writing as Rae Walsh
　　The Lost Art of Reverie: Aveline Book 1
　　A Jar Full of Light: Aveline Book 2
　　The Fire in our Hearth: Aveline Book 3

Reviews

Recommendations and reviews are such an important part of the success of a book. If you enjoyed this book, please take the time to leave a review.
　　Don't be afraid of leaving a short review! Even a couple lines will help and will overwhelm the author with waves of gratitude.

Contact

Email: racheldevenishford@gmail.com
　　Blog: http://journeymama.com
　　Facebook: http://www.facebook.com/racheldevenishford
　　Twitter: http://www.twitter.com/journeymama
　　Instagram: http://instagram.com/journeymama

www.ingramcontent.com/pod-product-compliance
Lightning Source LLC
Chambersburg PA
CBHW030251100526
44590CB00012B/365